THE
NICE
LITTLE
BLONDE
GIRL

LINDA FRANK

Cover design: Hilda Chen
From a 1912 painting of the Golden Rose Synagogue by Odo Dobrowolski
Interior formatting: Robin Krauss, www.bookformatters.com

ISBN: 978-0-9844939-3-7

To my granddaughter Mirah: This story is part of your heritage that I hope you never forget.

"She sits alone . . . With the fall of her people into the enemy's hand and none to help her, her enemies saw her and gloated at her downfall . . . God has delivered me into the hands of those I cannot withstand . . . My soul remembers well, and makes me despondent. Yet, this I bear in mind; therefore, I still hope."

The Book of *Lamentations*

"Nostalgia even likes to falsify flavours, too, telling us to taste nothing but the sweetness of Lwów today. But I know people for whom Lwów was a cup of gall."

Józef Wittlin

Prologue

Lwów, Poland
December 1936

A Jewish family reunion. By definition an event fraught with stress, sniping, and dispute. The occasion was the fiftieth wedding anniversary of parents in their seventies—but, as they did then, appearing decades older. Few couples of their generation celebrated this marital milestone. Which is why even the youngest of the three sons was persuaded, by his wife who had never met his family, to return to Lwów, pronounced Lvov, now Poland. This was the city he had left when it was called Lemberg, when it was part of the Austro-Hungarian Empire, the capital of which, Vienna, was where they and their six-year-old daughter lived. The Empire, like the German name Lemberg, had been lost nearly twenty years before. The name Lemberg would be restored to the city five years after this party by a conqueror avenging the defeats of both the Emperor Franz Josef and his neighboring colleague, Kaiser Wilhem II. This new tyrant would forever obliterate family reunions like this all over Europe.

The political and nomenclature evolutions of the hometown resonated in the strained relationships in this family. Its patriarch was Weinberg (pronounced *Veinberg*) the Watchmaker, or "*zigermacher*" in Yiddish, and his wife "the *alte*" Mrs. *V*einberg. In the polite circles of their age group, first names were rarely used socially. In the family they were *Tate* and Mama to the elder two sons and daughters-in-law who lived locally—one couple childless and the other parents of a son and daughter. And *Zayde* and *Bubbe* to those grandchildren. But the little girl from Vienna did not understand these names or why the children introduced as her cousins didn't call the grandparents Grandmama and Grandpapa, as she called Dr. Heilbron and his wife in Vienna. She had never really heard anyone speak Yiddish, except when her mother took her to the dressmaker shop in Leopoldstadt, a district a considerable distance from the elegant apartment building near the university and its prestitgious hospital where her father and maternal grandfather were distinguished "*herr doktors*." And why was everyone here calling her Papa "Yankel"? At home he was Jack.

The squabbling started when the middle brother and his wife, Chaim and Esther, arrived at the restaurant, one of Lwów's prized Kosher eateries. ("Ugh," said Yankel/Jack walking in, "who picks a restaurant for its famous gefilte fish?"). Chaim and Esther, followed by Shlomo, age twelve, and Chanah, age eight, sidled into the private dining room maneuvering a package about three feet tall and four feet wide, wrapped in brown paper tied with wide golden ribbon and an oversized bow. This was their joint anniversary gift with the other brother and wife, Nathan and Freya. Bubbe and Zayde cooed with appreciation after stripping off the wrapping. It was a painting of a peasant woman in the fields with her children, framed in heavy gilt with a small plaque engraved with the name of the artist: A. Kozakiewicz.

Jack could not restrain himself from hissing to his wife.

"How bourgeois! The painting and the frame. It's not like it's a Renoir—but even for a Renoir, how déclassé it would be to put the painter's name on it. See, Elisabeth, why I didn't want to come? My family—they're like peasants themselves."

"Shush," said his wife. "Your parents love the painting. And your family are not peasants. They're very nice and happy to see us. Finally, Lily gets to meet her other grandparents."

Despite her attempts to keep this exchange down to a whisper, Jack's tone attracted notice. And both brothers turned on him.

"You show up after twenty years and you're still the same *schmuck* you always were," said Nathan, the oldest, as his elderly parents and wife Freya gasped and tried to shut him up.

"No, Mama and *Tate*, this has to be said. You two—and Chaim and I helped—struggled to support him through university and medical training, and this is how he repays us all. We never asked for anything from you, Herr Doktor, because we knew better than to expect you to be a *mensch*."

Lily pulled on her mother's sleeve. "Why are they yelling at Papa? I don't understand. Tell me what's wrong."

Elisabeth, accustomed to rationalizing her husband's behavior—primarily to herself—pooh-poohed the fuss.

"Just grown-ups acting like children, Lily. Why don't you get to know your cousin Chanah? Maybe sing songs or something? Go talk to her before we sit down to dinner. Look how pretty she is, with that shiny blonde hair. She looks like a nice little girl like you, sweetheart."

PART I

Chapter 1

Only Simon Rieger, my significant other, would get mobile phone service effective enough to reach him while hiking through this breathtaking and historic recreational site deep in Israel's Negev desert. When the ring-tone jarred us both, even Simon seemed embarrassed by this piercing intrusion in this place, which was quiet, even meditative. But, to my chagrin, not embarrassed enough to ignore it or turn it off.

"Michael, I'm never too busy not to talk to you," he said loudly enough to ensure that conversation in a canyon could be heard. And would be overheard by other nearby hikers craving the peacefulness of the place. Fortunately, on this weekday in early winter, there were none.

We were at Timna, the site of ancient copper mines, dubbed "King Solomon's mines" by twentieth century archeologist and Reform Jewish rabbi and academic Nelson Glueck. The authenticity of that name remains unconfirmed, though copper mining in the vicinity likely existed in Solomon's time. The mine operation only ceased in 1985, giving way to recycling and modern manufacturing innovations. The Jewish National Fund project Timna Park has made the grandeur of the setting and its verified and theoretical history accessible to day-trippers, campers, and scholars alike.

Simon and I relished exploring this place in desert warmth after a week of rain when we first arrived in Israel. As New Yorkers, we can hardly complain about such mild winter weather, but the dampness and penetrating chill in Jerusalem and Tel Aviv equaled the rawness of trauma that preoccupied everyone we met still reeling from the assassination of Prime Minister Yitzchak Rabin less than a month before. This day at Timna, part of a three-day retreat to the Negev, was a perfect refuge from the unsettled mood in the cities. But, as Simon's conversation progressed, it seemed our time in this haven was to be a short-lived.

"Sure, sure. Ukraine, wow! The Vatican? Sure, I can go next week. Easily. Look, I'm not in a position to write down the details right now. Send me a fax to the Dan in Eilat. Yes, yes, the hotel is okay. No damage. People are just shaky, no pun intended."

Adding to Israel's national angst that November was an earthquake felt throughout the length of the miniscule country, but most profoundly in the resort city of Eilat, on the shore of the Red Sea Gulf of Aqaba, fifteen miles south of Timna. The seismic trembling originated beneath that body of water, though that did not prevent me from a dip off our hotel's beach when we arrived the day before. December in the Red Sea. Who could resist? Not a habitual swimmer like me.

From Simon's end of the conversation, I figured he had another assignment related to his expertise in old Jewish manuscripts and texts. The summons would come from the Mossad, Israel's Central Institute for Intelligence and Special Operations for which he occasionally moonlighted as a consultant, in addition to his diamond and jewelry business. Such requests usually meant a precious work with suspect provenance had turned up somewhere, a frequent occurrence since the Holocaust had upended European Jewish culture as systemically as it annihilated its population. Ukraine had recently emerged independent from the downfall of the Soviet Union. Looted art and Judaica long sequestered behind the Iron Curtain and the Berlin Wall were trickling into the marketplace. But a Vatican connection?

"Who's Michael? It wasn't Avi who called?"

Avi Ben Ze'ev was Simon's close friend and main contact in the Mossad.

"Michael is my friend at the Israel Museum. A restorer and quite the scholar himself. A manuscript, a codex from Lviv, has shown up in Rome, and the museum was asked to buy it."

"Asked by the Vatican?"

"Supposedly. Which is strange, because anything really valuable the Vatican would just quietly integrate into its own extensive Judaica collection without concern for us or provenance. Which is why Avi told Michael to call me. Which is why I'm going to Rome in a few days. You'll come with me, I hope."

Despite savoring the sunshine under a straw hat wearing only a short-sleeve shirt and light cotton pants—and craving more wintertime swims off the beach in Eilat—my curiosity and the smell of a good story led me to agree. I am, after all, a journalist by trade and training, albeit semi-retired, and I sniffed a potential piece. Ironically, it was on assignment, more than five years before, to investigate just such Judaica—emerging from the decades-old shadow of the former Soviet Union—that my "second career" as a benefactor for retrieving looted art began. That magazine assignment led me to an auction in New York and the first sighting of my family's antique Seder plate fifty-two years after the Nazis had carted it off, along with my father, in Vienna. Then came the hunt for the quickly withdrawn Seder plate, a quest that led toward several life-changing spin-offs: the revelation that I had a Chinese-Jewish Judaica scholar cousin in Israel, who now calls me "the Jewish Miss Marple"; the bequest from my surrogate Uncle Nachman Tanski, himself a renown Judaica and art collector; and the establishment of the foundation, from that inheritance, that helps looted art victims recover their treasures. That auction was fateful in one more way—I met Simon there.

"Okay. It's like heaven here. But Rome at this time of the year is probably more moderate than New York or Ukraine."

Chapter 2

Three days later, settling into the Excelsior Hotel on the *Via Veneto*, chosen by Simon for the indoor swimming pool he knew I'd use every morning, we received a delivery of flowers to welcome us. The extravagant bouquet of red roses came from one Father Gajos, a surname startling at first to us when thinking of the Vatican Italian stereotype but less so in the era of a Polish pope whose reign had already witnessed the demise of the godless Soviet bloc and the apparent revival of religion among its historically Catholic members. On the card the priest thoughtfully wrote we must be tired from our journey, wished us a pleasant first evening in Rome, and promised a phone call in the morning to confirm meeting and lunch the next day.

"That's nice," I said, "and such gorgeous roses in December. It seems the Vatican spares no expense when setting up a deal. Does the good Father know you're here to put the kibosh on a sale?"

"The whole thing is very fishy and atypical. If what we're going to see is a real find, the Vatican wouldn't be offering it for sale."

"So, the museum suspects it's a forgery?"

"The museum, and the Mossad. They don't know what to think. They're very suspicious simply because it's uncharacteristic—yet curious enough to follow up on the lead. The codex purports to be a previously unknown work of The TaZ. He was a major contributor to the *Shulchan Aruch*."

The *Shulchan Aruch*, I had learned, was a code of Jewish law widely adopted and adapted, through differing opinions of rabbinical commentators after its inception in the sixteenth century. The title means "the set table" in Hebrew. But that was the sum total of all I knew of what Simon was talking about. To say that the formal Jewish education of a young Viennese girl, born to an assimilated family and rescued by the kindertransport to wartime London, lacked depth is an understatement. Admittedly, living in New York City and frequently spending time in Israel, I had had plenty of opportunities to make up for it but directed my interests elsewhere. I always relished Simon's gently offered tutorials, though.

"The TaZ? Who or what's that? And how do you spell it?"

"Capitol *T*, lower case *a*, capital *Z*, was Rabbi David Samuel Ha-Levi Segal. He was a prominent rabbi and scholar in Galicia, which is now mostly in Ukraine, where this manuscript supposedly comes from. TaZ is an acronym of his most famous work, *Turei Zahav*. Turei, spelled with a *tet*, means Lines of Gold, a play on *turei* spelled with a *taf*, which refers to Towers of Gold in the Song of Songs. *Zahav*, of course, means gold. There are a lot of acronyms of scholarly names, like the RAMBAM. That's an acronym of Rabbi Moshe ben Maimon. Better known as Maimonides."

"Ah. I see. Interesting. I'm so impressed by what you know that I don't," I said to Simon, pulling him down on the bed for a kiss that might lead to more. "What would I do without you?"

"I keep telling you that, Lily, every time I ask you to marry me. I know, I know. Don't start with that sore point. Anyway, there's plenty about you that's impressive, my dear," he said, responding to my kiss. "Now, don't you think it's time for a little nap before our first dinner in Roma?"

Promptly at nine the next morning, opening the door to our room after forty minutes in the Excelsior's art-surrounded but smallish swimming pool, I heard Simon agreeing to meet Father Gajos at eleven-thirty.

"Yes, Father, of course, we can take a taxi. No need to send a car for us. We've been to Rome before. And every driver knows how to get to the Vatican, ha, ha . . ."

Two hours and twenty minutes later, in said taxi, we crossed the Tiber and turned toward St. Peter's Square. For me, neither Catholic nor even Christian—no matter that I had been there before—approaching the Egyptian obelisk and nearby fountains, framed by the semi-circle colonnade its genius designer Bernini called the outstretched arms of the Church, elicited a tingle of awe. The kind of wondrous appreciation I feel every time I cross one of the bridges into Manhattan or San Francisco, stroll along the Thames near the British Parliament, spot the Eiffel Tower from afar. Which makes me just a sucker for iconic postcards.

When the taxi turned right and circled around the back of St. Peter's, where, even in December tourists were lined up to enter the Vatican Museum, I was surprised we kept going and turned right again, away from the familiar Vatican sites into an adjacent neighborhood. The cab finally stopped on a corner, where the sight in front of us was the metal-fenced grass courtyard of a dirty beige brick church.

"Yes, this is it, *Via Angelo Emo*. We need to cross the street," said Simon, grabbing my elbow. "We're meeting him at his residence. It's that salmon-colored stucco building. Number five."

A tall oak double door and grey marble marked the entry of the four-story building. Overhead a shuttered central window bore a five-pointed star chiseled into its frame, and above that was a stone coat of arms, undecipherable at its distance and height. Less impressive was the contiguous commercial space housed in flat-roofed one-story attachments: a restaurant on one side and an auto and motor scooter repair shop on the other. The Vatican is nothing if not a practical landlord.

After pushing open the heavy door, we climbed a staircase one flight to a landing where a portly, bespectacled man, garbed in a black priestly cassock bearing a large metal cross on his ample midriff, stood watching us. I figured he was older than Simon and me, a man in his late seventies, at least.

"Mr. Rieger?"

"Father Gajos?"

"Just call me Father Stash, it's short for Stanislav. Please come in."

I was introduced as Simon's friend, and we stood idly in a small hallway as Father Stash scurried away. A woman of indeterminate age wearing a white apron over a shapeless grey dress, matched perfectly by her hair, appeared and nodded to us. After a few minutes the priest returned to the hall swinging a metal ring of keys.

"You must be hungry. Let's go to eat. Signora Margaretta, I will return by two."

So back down the staircase we went, Father Stash lumbering down the steps one leg at a time and wheezing heavily despite the slow pace.

"Knees," he said. "Arthritis. And emphysema. I'm afraid I succumbed to the temptation of the cigarette as a young man, and then the seemingly more aesthetic and scholarly pipe. It's too late to repair the damage, so why deprive myself at this age?"

On the sidewalk we turned right and went into the restaurant, where the apparent proprietor greeted the priest with a bear hug. The man was bearded and stooped over a cane but otherwise the very image of an elderly undertaker in an opaque jet-black suit.

"Franco, Signor Martelli, my dearest friend, these are my new friends from America. And Israel. Signor Rieger and Signora Kovner. It's a great occasion to welcome them."

Surrounded by florid murals depicting, on opposite walls, chariot races and toga-clad Roman orators addressing the masses, Franco, despite his immobile stance, oversaw the delivery of a scrumptious succession of courses separated by five-minute intervals: an antipasto platter of cheese, olives, and marinated vegetables and tuna ("no salami or prosciutto—I wouldn't insult my Jewish friends," said the priest.); tagliatelle ribbons topped by slivers of prized white truffle; baked cod in tomato sauce; herbed lamb chops; mixed green salad; and gelato with buttery amaretti cookies. All accompanied by white and then red wine and an ever-present basket of crusty bread.

Fortunately, the food belied the decor; it was indeed a wonderful lunch, and the lively conversation focused on this food and on food in general. The priest understandably savored Italian cuisine and expounded at length on its virtues compared to that of his native Ukraine.

Eventually, I tried to steer the discussion elsewhere. Journalism 101: open-ended questions.

"It must have been hard to be a priest in Ukraine, between the Nazis and the Communists."

"Oh, yes, signora. But I spent most of the war here in Rome. In fact, most of my career I have spent here. That is how I became acquainted with Franco Martelli. This restaurant has been in his family for two generations. Franco I met when I studied here. The Martelli family treated me like another son from the beginning. They figured they still had one son a priest even after Franco chose the restaurant business over the priesthood. That leg. Since the war never the same."

"How did your family back home react to your life so far away? I assume they stayed there?"

"My parents, of course, are long departed. They survived the war, and were happy their son could serve the church in a place where it was not just permitted but, of course, celebrated. I was able to visit them occasionally but traveled in civilian clothes when I did. But now it is nice to return to my roots, as you would say, to visit Lviv feeling free to go there as who I am—a man of the church. I travel there maybe once or twice a year. I have a sister remaining, with children and grandchildren. It is very special to be a grand-uncle."

Simon was fidgeting, his exasperation with the monologue palpable. I could see that getting to the point of the visit was more on his mind than building a rapport with Father Stash. Flashing him a look that he knew meant "hold it," I persisted.

"So, Father," I said, "you've been working in Rome since the thirties or forties? Doesn't it take years to become a priest? University, seminary? You don't seem old enough to have done all that before the war."

"Ah, signora, you flatter me. I'm seventy-five, the same age as our Holy Father, and half-Polish—on my father's side. You know, when I left Lviv, it was Lwów, part of Poland. To your question about my education, yes, I completed all my studies here in Rome."

"Lviv, Lwów—Galicia," I said. "My father came from there. He left when he was just a teen-ager, a student, and it was still called Lemberg during the Austro-Hungarian Empire. As far as I know he returned only once, with my mother and me, when it was Lwów, a few years before the second war. If you were Jewish, you'd be called a Galitzianer, and we would be *lanzmen*, people from the same place."

Father Stash laughed appreciatively. "Yes, you are so right."

Simon rolled his eyes signaling, "let's get to the point."

"Now this manuscript you've brought us here to see," I said. "It comes from Lviv? How does it happen that someone in your position, especially so long away from your homeland, has come into possession of a rare and possibly valuable text from a Jewish scholar of the seventeenth century?"

"Religious scholarship knows no boundaries or national borders. Let me show you what I have." With that, he hoisted himself off his chair, as the attentively lurking Franco reached into his pocket and produced a key chain holding only one key.

"Ah, finally," said Simon moving toward the door at the front of the restaurant.

The priest had turned the other direction, and was advancing toward the back of the dining room.

"This way," he said.

Simon, his hand on the doorknob, swung around in disbelief.

"What?" he said. "You mean we're not going to the Vatican Museum or one of its store room buildings?"

"Follow me," said Father Stash, his own key chain in hand, pointing us toward a narrow passageway past the kitchen. As we entered this corridor, I almost bumped into the protruding gold frame of a painting hanging next to a WC sign. The painting, a dense oil depicting a pastoral scene of a woman and children pitching twigs into a fire, looked familiar. The frame, baroquely detailed and heavy, bore an engraved label with the artist's name: A. Kozakiewicz.

"Father Stash," I said, "this painting. "It doesn't go with the decor of the restaurant. It's Polish, and I think I've seen it before."

"Oh, it's a gift from me to Franco. Brought to Rome by the same priest from Lviv who brought the codex I'm going to show you now. Kozakiewicz was a well-known painter in Poland in the last century, but his work is not especially sophisticated or respected. It appeals to bourgeois collectors. Even Franco has hung it in this hidden spot. I know he only put it up at all out of respect for me. It's not my taste any more than it is his."

As if the Roman gladiator scenes that must have been Franco's choice were fine art. Trying to remember where I had previously seen the Polish oil, I remained fixated in front of the painting as Father Stash led Simon farther down the back corridor and I heard a door open.

"Lily," said Simon, "come on. Why are you staring at that ghastly painting?"

"I've seen it before. I can't remember where or when. Okay, I'm coming."

Bourgeois. Peasants. The artist's name on the very fancy frame. Where had I seen it before? I strained to remember, charging the difficulty to a "senior moment." Reluctantly, I edged away and joined them in a plain room surrounded by chipping grey walls, furnished with a battered metal desk and chair, a five-foot filing cabinet, and a rickety wooden table squeezed into a corner. On it sat a box of incongruously pristine polished oak.

"This is Franco's office," Father Stash said. "Only he has the key."

"Why would you keep it here, instead of in a Vatican storage place or even your own residence?"

"Personal reasons."

With a large key from his ring he opened the box. In it was a thin book with a maroon leather cover clamped together by a silver filigreed clasp. Simon carefully lifted it out, set it on the table, and undid the clasp to reveal a loosely held sheaf of papers etched with Hebrew writing. He pored over the first page.

"Mr. Rieger," Father Stash said, "Stop and look closely at these first two or three pages. Do you see the signs of writing underneath? Do you think they were the scholar's notes or a first draft? The notes of another scholar? Either way, it looks like someone was trying to erase that writing and replace it."

Simon did not answer right away. He held the manuscript close up, gently rolled a finger over it, and tilted it underneath the dim light.

"Your impression is accurate, Father Stash. It's definitely a palimpsest. The Hebrew of the scholar is written over something else that wasn't entirely erased. Parchment and vellum were expensive, and people often tried to reuse it. Or there's something underneath that was deliberately obliterated for a reason. If, indeed, this is from The TaZ. That I'm not sure about either."

"What makes you doubt it? The gentleman who brought this to me emphasized the importance of Rabbi Ha-Levi and of his work, which I'm assured this is."

Father Stash looked petrified as if thinking he might be peddling the wrong Talmudic scholar to the Israel Museum.

"My only hesitation about attributing it to him," Simon explained, "is that this appears to be handwritten. Maybe it was a sermon, or whatever they called an address to the congregation then. I've never heard of any of his personal written work found. That said, if we can identify this as his, it would be amazing. In any case, what's underneath could be significant, too, but there are some Hebrew letters and the

Latin alphabet with Polish accent markings. You read Polish, Father Stash. Have you been able to make out any of it?"

"I really haven't had time to devote to this since it came into my possession," said the priest. "But, just from looking at it now, it looks like it would be quite a feat to decipher what's underneath."

My relationship with Simon had schooled me a bit in the jargon of historic Jewish texts, his passion in which he was very knowledgeable. I had learned that a palimpsest is text written over something else either for the practical reuse of the parchment or paper or to cover up what is underneath. Apparently, Father Stash also knew the term. This surprised, but strangely reassured, me.

"There are ways restorers, like Michael, my friend at the Israel Museum, can make the writing more visible," Simon said while snapping photos of the manuscript pages. When he was done he faced the priest and asked, "How exactly did you, or the priest from Lviv, come upon this?"

"He said it was in the belongings of his dear, departed mother."

"Why and how would a Catholic woman from Ukraine have a Hebrew manuscript, possibly the work of an important scholar, in her possession? It must have originally belonged to a Jewish collector or a synagogue or academy. Have you known this priest long? Did you know the mother?"

"The Duck, excuse me Father Kaczka—it's a joke, because the name means duck in Polish—is a priest I have known since he began his studies at seminary at the start of the war. He is several years younger than I am. I believe my parents knew his, but I left so long ago I don't remember the connection. He was trapped, so to speak, by the Soviet years, which cast a shadow on his career opportunities as a priest. It is hard to regain those years."

"So, he's trying to make a living by selling looted Judaica to Israel? And what is his price?"

"I wouldn't put it so crassly, Mr. Rieger. He is interested in what is fair value, and that amount would be donated to the Ukrainian church council in Lviv, which is in desperate need of funds. He believes the manuscript to be worth more than one million dollars—$1.3 million is the asking price, but I'm certain he would negotiate a bit."

Simon gave me a look that said oh, yes, I'm sure he'd negotiate.

"Wouldn't the Vatican be interested in this and try to help the Lviv church, as well?" he asked the priest. "If proved to be the authentic work of as well-known a Talmudic commentator as The TaZ, it's potentially of the quality and significance the Vatican itself collects. Especially if the content underneath proves to be anything unique and previously unknown. Not that the Vatican should be collecting work looted from Jews, but stranger things have happened."

"You're very cynical, aren't you, Mr. Rieger? Here is someone from Lviv, isolated from his faith for many years, offering something of value to the Jewish State, and you mock his intentions and, by insinuation, mine."

"I apologize, Father Stash," said Simon. "I believe you are acting in good faith and you have shown to Mrs. Kovner and me wonderful hospitality and graciousness. However, the Israel Museum doesn't purchase works of unknown provenance, and the provenance of this manuscript is very cloudy, to be charitable. In any case, I don't think it's worth $1.3 million. However, let me photograph it, and I will relay the information and our discussion to my client in Israel."

"Oh, my God," I blurted out as a sixty-year-old scene flashed back to me. Both Simon and Father Stash turned toward me not understanding. But some instinct led me to downplay my outburst.

"Oh, nothing. Sorry. Something just popped into my mind. Not important."

But it was. At that moment I remembered my grandparents' fiftieth wedding celebration in Lwów when I was six years old. That was when I had last seen that painting. It was a gift from my aunt and uncle to my grandparents. My father hated it. "Bourgeois" was what he called it. Just like Father Stash did. What was it doing on a stucco wall next to the toilet in this nondescript, albeit delicious, trattoria, within steps of the Vatican Museum and its certifiable treasures? It seemed as incongruous as was the supposedly million dollar scholarly codex locked in the restaurant's back room.

I had long assumed my father's side of my family had perished in the Holocaust, if I thought about them at all. I had escaped to London on the kindertransport in late 1938, and was taken in by my mother's sister and her husband, raised from the age of eight as part of their family along with their two sons. By that time my father had already died in Dachau, and my mother and maternal grandparents, who had remained in Vienna, met their fate as deportees "to the East" in 1941.

I learned this in 1945. Before I left Vienna in late 1938 my mother had been informed by the family in Lwów that the Galician grandparents I had met only once, at that auspicious golden anniversary party, had died of natural causes within months of each other. It was still several months before the Nazi invasion of Poland officially launched the war in September 1939. Lwów, where my father's family was, lay in eastern Poland, a chunk of Russia's portion in the carving up of Poland Hitler and Stalin agreed to just before the invasion. In another two years, during the summer of 1941, Hitler reneged on the deal and sent his forces sweeping eastward through Stalin's turf en route to Russia itself. My relatives might have survived at least until then. However, if this painting was really the same one, obviously no one in my family possessed it anymore. The same priest who had brought the questionable manuscript to Rome had also acquired a picture that had hung on the walls of a middle-class Jewish family. Mine. His mother's collection? How?

For the previous five years, after rediscovering my family's antique Seder plate, art looted from Jews by the Nazis and their henchmen throughout Europe had become a personal focus crystallized by the creation of my foundation dedicated to recovering such booty for survivors or their heirs. Was it possible that another vestige from my own shrunken family had landed on this wall in front of me?

I would tell Simon what my "aha" moment meant after we parted from Father Stash. The old cleric peddling the suspect codex from the back of a grungy trattoria now seemed to me to be just as sleazy as my vision of his younger disciple returned from wartime privation and Communist suppression to a revived life of faith. Something told me not to inject my personal discovery into the mix right now. Besides, maybe I was wrong. Maybe the oil painting was a hack commodity picture in Poland. I had no idea who the artist A. Kozakiewicz was.

"Father," I said, "where is this Duck whose mother left him the manuscript and the painting?"

"In fact, Signora, he is in Rome, and he is coming to my residence this evening to learn about our discussion here today. I am certain he will want to meet you and Signor Rieger. We can do that tomorrow. Let us again schedule for eleven o'clock in the morning. Father is an honorable man and means no harm. I am sure of that."

"Sometimes, harm comes from where you least expect it," I muttered softly enough to avoid a reaction from Father Stash.

"I wouldn't get your hopes too high, Father," said Simon. "However, we will take the time to meet 'The Duck.' See you tomorrow."

I could only nod as the priest bowed and extended his arm to indicate I should exit the storeroom first. Figuring out where I had previously seen the "bourgeois" painting pulled me mentally back sixty years to that other world and reminded me of the journey of that other object from that time and place, my family's treasured Seder plate. I ultimately learned it had been a pawn in a scheme that bartered military support for Israel's War of Independence for the free and prosperous postwar life of a Nazi war criminal. This was a diabolical deal engineered and carried out by my trusted surrogate relative, Nachman Tanski, from whom I inherited the source of my organization's funding. He had justified the deal as a treacherous means to a righteous end. While I might sometimes preach forgiveness to my still-bitter adult children, in my heart of hearts the betrayal continued to sting five years later.

Yet, by comparison, the motives of some unknown priest claiming his mother owned a valuable Jewish manuscript *and* my grandparents' painting were way too suspicious for polite benefit of the doubt. It would be interesting to meet The Duck.

And, as we bade Father Stash good-bye at his doorway, the enormity of seeing the painting and the disturbance that came from long-suppressed flashes of memory overcame me. I leaned on the pink stucco wall outside the apartment building and simply stood there immobile. Simon faced me and took both my hands.

"Now tell me, what was that outburst about? Obviously not nothing. About where you saw that picture before?"

"You know me too well. I think it was in Lviv, Lwów, whatever it's called, the one time we visited my grandparents on my father's side. It was their fiftieth wedding anniversary. My father wasn't on particularly good terms with his own family, but we did go to see them that one time. I think my mother really pushed him when the invitation came."

"Wow," said Simon. "You never talk about your father at all. Why didn't he get along with his family?"

"He rejected them as low-class, too Jewish, all the stereotyped objections of the sort of snob he became in Vienna, when he took on the value system he thought my mother and her family's milieu required. Let's just say he wasn't interested in dredging up his roots. Or even admitting to them."

"And this painting was in the grandparents' house? Is that how you remember it? Just from visiting once?"

"What I remember is its grand entrance to the anniversary dinner, which was in a restaurant. I think there were two sets of aunts and uncles, my father's brothers and their wives, and a couple of kids. They carried the painting side-ways into the room where the party was."

"Grand entrance. It definitely sounds like one. Did everyone applaud the effort when they got it in?"

"The grandparents were thrilled and loved the picture. But my father didn't and touched off—well, I guess now we'd say World War III. It was about 1936, so there had only been the one Great War by then. Anyway, he started a huge row when he made a comment, in not exactly a stage whisper, about how bourgeois this painting was."

"Well, it is. And then what happened?"

"The brothers lit into him. All I remember was my mother fretting about it and trying to distract me by pushing me to play with another little girl, who must have been my first cousin, the daughter of one of the brothers. She was either my age or maybe a little bit older. She had an older brother, too, twelve or thirteen. I was only six. I don't even remember their names."

"Depending on our meeting with The Duck and if you really think this picture belonged to your grandparents, do you want to go to Lviv to pursue this and try to find out what happened to your aunts and uncles and the cousins?"

"I don't know if I can bear another trip to my yesteryear to get to the bottom of this."

"You and Ruth counsel people with looted belongings all the time," Simon reminded me.

It was true. Through Uncle Nachman's fortune I had helped many Holocaust survivors and their heirs trace, identify, and reclaim Nazi booty. My cousin Ruth Sofaer, a Judaica scholar, led its work.

"But another chapter of my own family? I don't know. Especially after the last time. Maybe I should just walk into the restaurant and take the painting."

Simon looked shocked.

"Just kidding," I said. "I don't even like it. Just what it might represent."

"Your father's family was from Lwów, right? Unless this was a stock painting, a dime a dozen, how many families would have had one? Maybe, as Father Stash said, this A. Kozakiewicz was a well-known Polish artist and wasn't a complete hack turning them out like street painters. Maybe he was famous enough for others to copy. Though, somehow, I doubt that. But Polish painters aren't exactly my forte."

I sighed and said, "Nor mine. Oh, where is Uncle Nachman when we need him? This is hardly his taste, but he was knowledgeable about Polish art. I think he collected Maurycy Gottlieb, who painted Jewish life. Let's go back into the restaurant."

"Okay, but you're not seriously thinking about just taking it off the wall, are you?"

"It's tempting, but no. With the WC next to it, I have the excuse to check it out again. And you have your camera. I'd appreciate a discreetly taken photograph."

Another look, with a lugubrious and suspicious Franco observing us, only served to stoke both the pain and the mystique of recreating the past. I really did not crave the painting itself. It wasn't my taste, though I involuntarily cringed at the memory of my father criticizing it while my mother tried to squelch him. In the case of our Seder plate, there was no mystery about whether or not the Nazis had looted it. I was there.

"I don't know," I said to Simon when we were back on the street outside the restaurant. "Maybe I'm imagining that I ever saw this painting before. It was all so long ago, and I was very young. What's your thinking about the manuscript?"

"Well, the museum's not going to buy it, that's for sure. It could be a piece by The TaZ. Or not. If authentic, it's certainly looted. I will have to see what my 'masters' in Israel want me to do. We'll know more when we meet—what did Father Stash call him?—The Duck from Lviv in the morning. For now, what do you want to do? Go back to the hotel?"

"Let's walk, maybe to the ghetto."

"Why? Haven't you been? It's not such a short walk and it's the wrong direction from going back to the hotel," said Simon.

"I don't know. I just feel like it. And we did have a pretty big lunch," I reminded him. "The exercise will do us good."

"Forty minutes of swimming wasn't enough?"

"That was *my* exercise," I said, patting his slightly protruding paunch. "Besides, I need the air to clear my head. It's chilly, but crisp, and we're dressed warmly enough."

Chapter 3

The ghetto in Rome is an area of about ten square blocks along the Tiber across from the gentrifying Trastevere district. Anchored by a large synagogue, its main market street and winding lanes have remained shabbily intact, its density and tenement-like housing a far cry from the grandeur of the Vatican, despite the touristy commercialism that has attached to the historic home of Roman Jews in recent years.

Of the city's seven thousand Jews before the Holocaust, two thousand perished. There are plaques around the ghetto identifying homes where Nazi victims lived before the war, as well as the one in the piazza where more than a thousand Jews were gathered to be deported to Auschwitz. This plaque reads: *"On October 16, 1943, here began the merciless rout of the Jews. The few who escaped murder and many others, in solidarity, pray for love and peace from mankind and pardon and hope from God."*

Both Simon and I had poked around the district in our pasts, not together. My desire to go there from the meeting with Father Stash stemmed from some sort of nostalgia and an inclination to mingle, even anonymously, with my people, whether the people wandering around the ghetto were actually Jewish or remotely considered me one of them. I wasn't looking to *kvell* over the cultural quaintness or to eat the signature fried artichokes. Just be there for a bit, in that district where people had experienced what my family had. To grab, if possible, a sense of shared history of loss and survival. I try not to immerse myself in that, but it's always there, without my purposefully summoning it, in varying degrees of my consciousness. Any spark of memory whisks me back to pondering the fundamentals of my childhood, sometimes joyfully, but mostly with melancholy.

"Let's at least have some coffee or tea. This dampness is penetrating," said Simon as we walked down from the main entrance toward the business area.

Sidewalk seating was readily available at the many cafés, since this was a day to go inside, and we chose one that was less dingy than others. Tea is not the drink of choice among Italians, but I managed to wangle a cup of hot water with fresh mint and lemon from the young female server who was more enthusiastic about Simon's order of a *caffè normale* and almond biscotti. While it made her happy, I raised an eyebrow to Simon.

"What?"

"We did have dessert with lunch, you know."

"We did. But that was two hours ago. When in Rome . . . Got to have something to dunk in the coffee. If you're not going to marry me, you don't have the right to nag me."

"Whew. I'd like to think I'm trying to help you stay healthy to keep us enjoying life, not nagging. But that told me."

"Sorry, Lily. A little biscotti is not going to kill me. No fat in it. Minimal sugar. Look, the man at the next table is talking on a cell phone just like mine."

"Deft subject change," I said. "He's practically the only person I've seen in Rome with a cell phone at all."

This was a gentleman about our age with wavy silver hair and beautifully turned out in a well-cut grey suit and maroon-and-black patterned silk tie. Very suave. His call ended, he turned to us.

"I couldn't help but overhear," he said, "as my wife counsels me all the time as to what to order. But, like you signora, she is right. We should all be grateful, signor, don't you think, if the women in our lives want us to stay healthy?"

"You are right, sir," said Simon. "I noticed that you have a cell phone like mine. One doesn't see too many people using any in public. Yet."

"Indeed. Now that I have one, I don't know how I lived without it all my life and I suspect you and I are the tip of the iceberg before the rest of the world has them, too. Especially if the cost goes down."

"Which no doubt it will, as the scale of use rises. Why don't you join us? My name is Simon Rieger, and this is Lily Kovner. We are from New York."

"Thank you," the other man said as he moved his chair to our table. "My name is Jacobo Basevi. What brings you to Rome at this time of year? Not exactly tourist season. Business?"

"In a sense," said Simon. "A project."

"And what business are you in, signor, if I may ask?"

"Jewelry, diamond trading. And you?"

"I am an *avvocato*, a lawyer, as you would say. I specialize in property transactions. In fact, I just met with a client looking to buy and renovate buildings in the ghetto. Believe it or not, this area will soon undergo a resurgence and become a costly place to buy or rent. Some of our poorest Jews still live here. Ironically, those who own are sitting on gold mines. Those who don't won't be able to afford the rent or could be evicted because of renovation."

"I can believe it," I said. "Like the lower East Side in New York City, where the former tenements are now worth a fortune. Are some of the current owners or tenants original or long-time residents or their families?"

"The ghetto is a mixture of Jews and non-Jews. Of course, we lost many Jewish souls in the war. Jews now live all over the city, but not all are even Italian. Many families are Libyan, in fact, who came here after the Six Day War."

"In the States we've begun to use the term 'gentrification,' what happens to old neighborhoods that acquire more middle-class features like galleries and 'in' restaurants, often to the detriment of the original residents and local culture," said Simon. "Not that I blame you, sir, for representing clients engaged in such business. Business is business."

"Indeed, signor, and thank you. I'd like to think my clients are undertaking projects that will at least preserve the character and uniqueness of the ghetto and I hope make it possible for regular people to still live here. And you, signor Rieger, is it the jewelry trade that brings you and this lovely lady here? I have some excellent contacts in that industry here."

"Not exactly," said Simon. "Not this trip. All I can say is I'm on an errand of historical significance for some Israeli associates. And please call me Simon."

"Ah! Mysterious. And I am Jacobo, by the way. Do know that my family has been in Rome for many generations, so if I might be of service in introducing you to some of the elders of the community, please allow me to help. Whatever your mission is. I suspect you and Signora Kovner are well-travelled, so no doubt this is not your first visit to Rome. You have probably seen all the major sites, but, if you might be students or tourists of history, here for historic reasons, do you know about the *Fosse* Ardeatine massacre?"

"I have read a bit about it, Jacobo," I said. "Weren't some of the ghetto Jews taken to caves and slaughtered there?"

"Yes, *fosse* means caves. It was not solely a massacre of Jews, although seventy-five were Jewish. It was a reprisal for a resistance bombing that killed thirty-three German-speaking policemen from South Tyrol, an area of Austria both Italy and German had annexed over the years. They became Nazi policemen stationed in Rome. Ten Italian men were to be killed to avenge each of the thirty-three policemen. The victims were political prisoners already sentenced to death, as well as others simply in jail. To get to the number three hundred thirty, men were literally dragged off the streets, some as young as teen-agers. Eventually, they assembled five more than the quota, but they killed the extras, too, not wanting to leave behind any witnesses."

"Yet another horrific German crime," Simon said. "Why do you mention it, Jacobo?"

"I had an uncle among the victims. He was in the Resistance and probably did play a part in the bombing. For my family visiting the *fosse* is like visiting the gravesite or monument of a loved one."

"Like Yad Vashem for me," I said. "The Nazis killed my parents and one set of grandparents, at least. Just today I've been reminded of other relatives who must have also died in the Holocaust."

"Today? Here in Rome?"

"It's a long story," I said. "And I'm not even sure what it is."

"What I'm wondering, Signora Kovner and Simon, is if you would have time and be interested in visiting the *fosse* while you are in Rome. Perhaps tomorrow? I have no appointments in the afternoon and would be delighted to pick you up and escort you there. You seem like people whose interests here are not limited to *la dolce vita*."

"We have an appointment at eleven o'clock that will possibly include lunch afterward," said Simon, "so I'm not sure about the timing. Nor do I know exactly how long we will be staying in Rome. Perhaps we will leave the day after tomorrow."

"I understand," said Jacobo. "The *fosse* are a twenty-minute drive from the central part of the city. We don't want to go too late, as it gets dark early at this time of year. Why don't we say this? Let us exchange business cards and cell phone numbers. I will call you about noon to see how your meeting is going, and about lunch. If our arrangement will not work, I understand, but perhaps we can make another plan during your visit."

"I think that sounds like a plan itself," I said. "Don't you, Simon? I would like to visit the caves. And, Jacobo, please call me Lily."

"Of course, Lily," our new friend said, "then I shall look forward to speaking with you tomorrow and hope we can meet again. I know my wife would enjoy your company, too."

He got up and bowed before leaving the café.

"Very charming, don't you think?"

"If he's for real," said Simon.

"What do you mean? What's not for real?"

"I don't know. You're right. Why wouldn't he be? You know me. Not always so trusting. Even when I should be. Probably just the type. Suave Italian guy oohing over my Lily."

"Not exactly," I said with rolled eyes.

At that moment Simon's cell phone rang.

"Michael," he said. "Yes, we're in Rome. Yes, what we saw certainly belonged to someone besides this contact, if it's not forged. In fact, it's mildly interesting both because of whom I think was the scholar and because of what's underneath. It's a palimpsest . . . I can hear you salivating. But you're not going to buy it, for sure, with no provenance, and I told the priest this. I did take some great photos with your special camera. We're going back tomorrow to meet with the person who brought it to him from Ukraine. Eleven in the morning here . . . great . . . speak to you tomorrow."

"Michael loves a good restorers' mystery. Deciphering a palimpsest is a thrill for him. I can't say I blame him," said Simon. "Of course, compared to my travels with the 'Jewish Miss Marple,' . . .

"Cute," I said. "I wish I could say pursuing my mysteries was so much fun. With bad guys and personal angst, it's not like sitting in a lab with infrared lights or whatever your friend Michael uses to work his magic. Since seeing that painting today, I'm wondering if I've stumbled on another quest. And if I can put myself through it again."

"Come on," said Simon. "It's getting late. Let's walk around here a little more, then go to the riverside and get a cab back to the hotel. We will see what happens tomorrow. If nothing else, we should get some clarity from The Duck and maybe an interesting outing with Signor Smooth, our new pal Jacobo."

Chapter 4

Promptly at eleven the next morning we climbed the stairs in Father Stash's building and rang the bell at the entrance to his apartment. And rang again and again until finally Signora Margaretta, her eyes red from crying, opened the door a crack.

"Good morning, Signora," said Simon. "We have an appointment with Father Stash."

"Oh," she screamed. "*Morto*! Dead!"

"What? When?"

"Signor and signora, this morning he did not wake up when I brought his coffee tray. I knocked and knocked. No sound. I went in. No wake up."

I asked if he was ill last night.

"No, okay," she said. "Other padre came to visit. I brought vodka for them to drink. Padre Stash said thank you, go to bed . . ."

Simon said, "What other padre? A friend you knew?"

"Russian or Polish. Funny name, Padre Stash called him. The bird? The chicken? I can't remember."

"The Duck? From Ukraine."

"Si, signor, si. Duck."

I asked, "Did you hear anything they said? Were they arguing?"

"No, I don't listen. Never listen. Holy men, holy talk. Not my business. But, oh, Padre Stash, good man. I will miss him. And where will I go? So nice here."

Her wailing attracted the attention of other tenants in the building, and we could hear other doors opening to check out the source of the commotion.

"Can we come in?"

Simon looked at me quizzically. What did I think we were going to do in there?

The housekeeper thought a moment and opened the door just enough for us to slither inside the apartment.

"Father Stash," I said, "is he still here for us to pay our respects?"

"Oh, no," Margaretta said, "the Vatican doctor came, and the funeral man. They take him away at nine o'clock."

"What did the doctor say? Why did Father die?"

"Doctor said too much pasta maybe heart attack."

She gestured with her hand on her heart.

I looked around and saw two glasses on a table between a pair of large wing chairs in the priest's study.

"Where did Father Stash sit? Which chair?"

"This one," she said, sinking into it herself. "Oh, mio padre . . ."

I smelled both glasses. They smelled like diesel fuel. I made a face, and Simon laughed.

"Miss Marple and the tale of the poisoned vodka?"

"Whew. This is strong stuff. Is there such a thing as thousand proof?"

"I don't think so," he said, "but from where they come from at least the vodka is the real McCoy. Will there be an autopsy?"

Signora Margaretta looked puzzled.

"Examination of the body. Post mortem," I said.

"I do not know," she said. "The Church handles everything. Probably no reason. Old man. Could die anytime."

"Signora," I said, "Father Stash took us to the restaurant back room to show us a book we were going to buy. He stored it there for safekeeping. Perhaps you could find his keys so we can see if it's still there."

"He always kept keys over here," she said, leading the way to an antique chest on the wall opposite the two chairs. When she opened it, she gasped.

"They're gone. I saw him put the key chain away when he returned from your meeting yesterday. Never went out again after that. Never . . ."

"Not a surprise," Simon to me *sotto voce.* "Let's get out of here and go next door."

We thanked the still distraught Margaretta, who was relieved to back us out of the apartment.

Through the window of his restaurant we could see Franco sitting at a table toward the back, smoking and drinking red wine with a bottle in front of him. The door was locked, even though the place had been open at exactly the same time the day before. We knocked and waved until he came and opened it. He did not seem happy to see us.

"Oh, Signor and Signora, I'm sorry. But I'm not opening today. Told cooks no work for lunch. Maybe later. Dinner. Good-bye."

He looked like he had neither slept nor attended to any personal hygiene since we had seen him the day before. He wore the same slick suit, now wrinkled and stained, with tie undone and askew, beard untrimmed, hair greasy and falling onto his forehead. We assumed he had already heard about Father Stash.

"Franco," I said. "We share your grief. We are so sorry to hear about the padre."

"Thank you. Stash, my friend for so long. Dead. I can't believe it."

"Can we come in?"

He looked up and down the street and into the restaurant before opening the door just enough to let us in. He pointed to his back table and put two more glasses on it.

"Sit down, have some wine with me."

It was a little early for me without benefit of pairing with a meal like yesterday's lunch, but the occasion seemed to require at least some sipping.

"Apparently," said Simon, "Father Stash died during the night. His housekeeper found him dead this morning. She said the doctors figure it was a heart attack."

"Yes," said Franco, "Margaretta told me. He liked his food—cheese, meat, all the things the doctors say don't eat. But so quickly. He didn't seem sick yesterday. Oh, my God. I can't believe it."

"Franco," I said, "Forgive me, but you look like you haven't slept, maybe haven't changed your clothes since yesterday. Yet, you only found out about Father Stash this morning."

"Signora, you are very observant. That guy, the padre from Ukraine. If he really is a priest. No good. I knew it from the day he brought that box here. He was here last night, very late. I was locking front door to go home. He pushed the door open. Insisted I stay and drink with him. Go get special bottle from the cellar. 'Your best bottle,' he says. I go downstairs, come back, he's gone. The back room door open, the box gone. Even that ugly painting off the wall. Too late to call Stash on the phone. I know he likes to go to bed by ten. Margaretta would yell at me. I stayed here all night. Worrying. Too much wine. Look at me, I know I look like a tramp. Father Stash trusted me to keep that book safe. This morning I call to tell him the news it is gone, and she cried, tells me *he* is gone. I swear, that man killed my padre. Somehow."

Despite the distressing circumstances, I secretly found some personal validation that Franco shared my initial suspicions. Which Simon had pooh-poohed.

"Why do you say that?"

"The guy, The Duck, what Stash called him, was raving, angry when he came in here. Screaming and yelling about being tricked and two-timed. 'These people don't know what they're talking about,' he said. 'Jews. Cheap. Don't recognize value when they see it. Always looking for a better deal.' Sorry. I mean no harm, no insult to you. This is just what he said."

"You think he killed Father Stash because of us?" I asked.

"Well, at least he must have upset Stash enough for the heart attack. I don't know. Just a bad guy. Margaretta didn't like him either. She was devoted to Stash. Protective. Also very smart when it comes to people. Good instincts."

"Yes," Simon said. "Probably working for him was a good place for her, too. Now she's worried about her future."

"Margaretta is my cousin. Her husband died age forty, automobile accident. He was also friend of Stash since we were young men. But her son makes good living, owns two apartment buildings. Good boy. He will take care of her. No need to worry about Margaretta."

At that moment Simon's mobile phone rang.

"Ah, Jacobo. Yes, good morning . . . Oh, you're right. Almost afternoon . . . hmm. Let me check with Lily . . . please hold the line . . ."

Simon muffled the receiver with his hand and turned to me.

"He's calling about the trip to the cave. I almost forgot about that," I said.

"Yes. Do you want to go?"

"Why not? We don't have anything else to do this afternoon, and, with Father Stash and The Duck gone, we don't know what our plans are. Anyway, it's too late to try to leave today."

Simon returned to the phone.

"Okay, Jacobo, yes, it will be our pleasure to see this important place. Where to meet? . . . Oh, I see . . . Yes. We can do that. Our hotel, one-thirty."

"Franco, we have to go. Here is my card," Simon said, "with the number of my mobile phone. Thank you for the wine and for the discussion. And for caring for the book. It is not your fault it is gone. Please call me if there is anything you need or if you learn more about Father Stash's death or The Duck."

Franco got up and shook Simon's hand and kissed mine. "Go in peace, my friends. Good luck."

"Now I'm the one who needs to walk a bit, then we can grab a cab back to the hotel before Jacobo comes," said Simon. "It's only noon, just an hour since we arrived to see Father Stash. It feels like three a.m. What an intense morning!"

We started down the street and headed toward the Vatican Museum around the back of St. Peter's. Despite the chilly overcast, tourists were lined up as if it were a balmy spring day.

"So," I said, "now what? With Father Stash dead, the codex gone missing, and The Duck possibly responsible for both, do you want to stay in Rome or go somewhere else in Italy, back to Israel, home to New York?"

"I'm going to have to get back to Michael at the museum and to my masters in Israel. I talked to Avi for a few minutes when you were down at the pool this morning. The codex is obviously a looted piece, and Ukraine and its sister former Soviet Union countries are still fresh territory for recovery after so many years of isolation."

"Literally behind a curtain," I said. "I spoke to Ruth this morning, too. When you were in the shower. She said the foundation has had absolutely no claims from Ukraine on looted Judaica or any other art."

"Interesting. But not surprising. Those Jews who survived probably didn't go back. If there was a choice."

"Or, if they're still there, the years under the Communists would have stifled religious practice, Jewish or otherwise. Younger generations possibly don't even know they're Jewish. You heard what Father Stash said about The Duck and the difficulties the Church had all those years."

"Yes, The Duck," said Simon. "Although I wonder what kind of a priest he is. If he's really a priest. After what Franco said. Poor Franco. Having the loot whisked away under his watch and losing his friend, too. Although I don't think he cared much about the disappearance of the painting, considering the spot where he hung it. Next to the bathroom."

"The painting. Yes. The one that might be my grandparents' painting."

Simon stopped short and moved in front of me on the sidewalk, taking my hands into his.

"Lily, oh my God, how thoughtless I've been. Going on about the codex, the museum, Michael, Avi. What they want. Do you want to find out if that was the painting in your grandparents' house? Or how The Duck came by it? We can do that, no matter what the Israelis want me to do."

I hugged him.

"Forget it. I'm not mad at you at all. I haven't given that painting much thought since we saw it. It's nothing compared to the Seder plate at the auction—where we met. It's not anywhere near comparable in my memories, never mind its monetary value. Which wasn't the issue when I went looking for the Seder plate, anyway."

"I know that," said Simon. "But the family. You lost touch. Maybe there is someone left on your father's side."

"I only met my father's family that one time. I vaguely remember my grandparents and aunts and uncles and those cousins. They were Weinbergs, my maiden name. I suppose I could check at Yad Vashem, but Weinberg is hardly an uncommon name, and wasn't Lviv, Lwów, Lemberg—whatever it was called at different times—a fairly large center of Jewish life?"

"Yes, not as big a Jewish population as Warsaw or Vienna, but the center of eastern Poland or western Ukraine, depending on who was in charge and where the borders were at any given time."

I sighed. "It's more of a needle in a haystack than finding the Seder plate."

"Why do you say that? You didn't have a lot to go on when I met you that fateful day at the auction."

"You're right, I guess. But Uncle was still alive. Even though I didn't know he would figure into the story as much as he did, he knew Simon Wiesenthal, which was a little useful, and he was still connected in the Judaica world, which ultimately wasn't. But this. The painting alone isn't much of a lead. Who knows? That artist—A. Kozakiewicz—could have been some Polish hack. Although it's hard to believe my family would have framed it in such a grand way. As garish and overdone as that frame is, it must have been expensive, even then. It occurs to me, I'm not sure how, that one of the aunts and uncles might have owned a gallery and ordered it specially for my grandparents' anniversary gift."

"But, Lily, do you want to pursue it? Forget the painting. Do you want to find out what happened to your family there? If it's possible, now that Ukraine is more accessible."

"I just don't know. To put myself back onto that emotional rollercoaster again. It took me a long time to recover after the search for the Seder plate. And the repercussions of what I found out about Uncle. My kids' reactions. Both about him and their concern for me. On the other hand, it did change my life in some positive ways."

He laughed. "Yes. Such as?"

"Well, I did find a cousin I didn't know I had. Who is now my partner in doing wonderful work for others whose family treasures were looted. Oh, and there's this guy I met!"

I gave Simon a peck on his cheek. Right there in the shadow of St. Peter's Cathedral.

"Yes, well, there's no need to find another guy this time. But, who knows? Maybe there is another cousin out there you don't know about."

"Maybe. But I'm not sure I want to go to Ukraine to look."

By this time we had walked around the main piazza and were headed down the *Via della Conciliazione* toward the Tiber. A few restaurants and cafés were serving. I was hungry.

"Why don't we get a quick bite around here or go back to the hotel for something before Jacobo picks us up? It's only twelve-fifteen. That little place looks okay and busy enough but not jammed. We should be able to get in and out."

"Fine," said Simon. "You know I can always eat. Especially when in Rome."

He took my arm to cross the street. Just as we stepped off the curb on a corner, with a green light in our favor, a tiny blue Fiat we hadn't seen or heard turned from the side street on our left at a speed more appropriate for the *autostrada*. Simon yanked my arm, and we stepped back just time to avoid being hit. The car then stopped abruptly in the middle of the avenue and started to back up diagonally toward us, a move only halted by the appearance of a Vatican policeman who darted between us and the vehicle, brandishing a gun in his outstretched hand. The driver's reaction was to quickly shift forward and drive away.

The policeman shook his head and turned to us. "Are you all right, signor and signora? I apologize on behalf of Vatican City. Crazy driver. Not a local license plate. They think we don't patrol, that they get can away with murder here."

"I hope they don't, officer," I said.

He put his hands together as if in prayer, smiled and saluted us, then moved on.

"Look," I said to Simon, "there's a cab. Let's get out of here and have our bite to eat near the hotel. I'm done with Vatican City right now."

"Fine with me. I'm wondering if that driver's move was deliberately aimed at us. It could have been The Duck or one of his associates."

"Literally getting away with murder? Simon, are you becoming the Jewish Sherlock to my Miss Marple? Backing up toward us did look deliberate. We dodged him, whoever it was, but the possible murder I wonder about is that of Father Stash. We will probably never know."

"Unless it was The Duck driving that car, and he finds us again," said Simon.

"You've been reading too many mysteries."

"None quite like the real ones you've led me to," he said.

Chapter 5

An hour later, fueled by a shared pizza and small carafe of red wine, we greeted Jacobo as he pulled up to the Excelsior entrance in a sleek black Maserati Quattroporte sedan and popped out of the driver's seat to pump our hands and open the back passenger doors for us.

There was a woman sitting in front. She stared straight ahead, a black coat collar snug around her neck. We could see silver-streaked black hair tightly pulled into a chignon, the better to showcase highly polished silver and black onyx door-knocker earrings. But, once we got into the car, she turned around, smiled warmly, and extended her hand to each of us separately.

"I am Zosia, Jacobo's wife," she said. "He told me of the charming couple from New York he met yesterday. I decided to change an appointment to accompany you today."

"Delighted you did," I said. I couldn't place her accent, which, like her name, was not Italian. "May I ask where you're from?"

"Poland," she said. "Warsaw. Have you been?"

"Yes," Simon and I answered simultaneously and looked at each other, wondering when. Not with each other. I spoke first.

"I was there once with my late husband, who had a conference. He was an economist. This was in the late eighties, when the governments in Eastern Europe were becoming very interested in western economic practices."

"I had business there in 1990. A project," Simon said.

"Project." Code for a Mossad assignment.

"Dare I ask, Zosia," I said, "when did you leave?"

"1939. In the summer. I was twelve years old. My family and I went on holiday to meet relatives who lived in Lwów. On August 16 we all arrived at a resort where we stayed in cottages. My parents, my little sister—she was five—and my aunt and uncle and their baby boy. We planned to go home August 30. By then my parents knew Hitler was coming to Warsaw any day. What I didn't know was that they planned not to go home. They had sold many possessions to raise cash. My father was a dentist and he had already arranged to work for an older dentist in Lwów, where my aunt and uncle lived. It was part of Poland then but did not seem to be so much in harm's way as Warsaw. And where else was there to go? So, we moved there after the vacation. In retrospect it turned out to be folly but it somehow made sense to my parents. I suppose, when they learned during the vacation that Hitler and Stalin divided up Poland, they figured they had played the gamble just right. Not that Stalin was an angel, and many Jews were murdered by the Russians then or deported to Siberia, but at least in the eyes of a child—this child—life was pleasant enough until Hitler double-crossed Stalin two years later. The Ukrainians, of course, were anti-Semitic enough. The Nazis arrived and sat back and watched the welcome the local people gave them: such a pogrom—men and women walking down the street attacked and stripped naked, forced to scrub the pavement, kiss statues of Lenin. Ridiculous humiliation. Then so many taken to jail and shot dead. It was just the beginning of the nightmare. We were trapped. My parents' big bet a bust. As it turned out, those deported to Siberia were luckier. Most of them survived the war. Who could have predicted?"

"What a coincidence. My father's family lived in Lwów. As far as I know, no one survived."

"Very likely, I'm afraid," said Zosia. "I'm the only survivor in my family." She reached back again, pulled off her black leather glove, and pushed up the sleeve of her black cashmere coat, revealing a line of inked numbers on the inner side of her left wrist.

"Everyone else died with these on their arms."

What more was there to say? I reached over and gently took Zosia's hand. She smiled before withdrawing it and turning back to watch the road.

Listening to her story from the moment we had driven out of the hotel driveway and turned left onto the *Via Veneto*, I had lost track of our route. I suddenly realized we were driving around the Colosseum. I then asked Jacobo how long it would take to get to the caves.

"About fifteen more minutes, depending on the traffic, Lily. But it is an interesting trip, don't you think?"

"The scenery, yes. And Zosia has made it even more so," I said.

Exactly fourteen minutes later, after leaving urban Rome and driving into a forested area, we arrived at the parking lot of *Fosse Ardeatine*. Courtly Jacobo first opened our back door and helped me out of the car. Zosia remained inside until he did the same for her. We waited as perfectly tailored black wool pants and low-heeled leather boots emerged one leg at a time and she stood up grasping the top of the car window. When Zosia stepped down we saw that one leg was shorter than the other by at least two inches.

Opening her arms wide with a flourish, as if to greet a crowd on stage, she said, "What do theatre people say? Break a leg? The Nazis gave that new meaning. I used to get shoes and boots specially made to even things out but I'm too old to bother with that now. Let's go. It's cold just standing here."

She forged ahead leading the rest of us.

We entered the courtyard that fronts the scene of this infamous Nazi crime, an abandoned quarry with stone caves and tunnels topped by an oddly grassy roof over the entrance that looked like a man's ill-fitting toupée. The bronze gate evokes comparison to concentration camp barbed wire entwined into a figurative Tree of Life and transforming into outstretched human limbs bent at the stiff angles representative of death. An imposing concrete statue depicts three males, bound together as one standing figure, hands tied in back. Their faces reflect different ages—teen to elderly—and each looks toward a different element of the memorial—the burial place, the antiquated quarry cave, the peaceful courtyard—with etched expressions of their likely emotions as they approached their fate. One shows despair, another seems resigned with half-closed eyes, the third stares defiantly. Memorial plaques speak as if from the victims themselves.

Retracing their steps through the courtyard into the cavern entrance gave me the familiar feeling of entering so many Holocaust memorials and visiting a few camps. What a ritual it had become to visit these sites. I have always hoped such excursions were trips of honor and respect while never taking cavalierly my own good fortune as a Jewish child from Vienna. I had arrived to this place in a luxury sedan from a luxury hotel; more than three hundred innocents had been roughly transported here in crude trucks within minutes of being rounded up, mostly at random on the street, to meet a German vengeance quota.

Jacobo proved to be a well-informed guide. Somehow, he managed a straightforward historical narrative, despite his obvious emotional connection to the place. He first reminded us of the stage of the war in Italy at the time of the massacre.

As Germany's Axis partner, Italy escaped German invasion and occupation until 1943, when Mussolini was deposed as leader of the government and military. Hitler dramatically rescued Il Duce but, with the Allies advancing into the country, had to fill the power gap by dispatching his own forces to take over the Fascist fight against them.

However, the Italian Resistance was well established by March 23, 1944, when it bombed a column of Tyrolean military policemen marching in *Via Rasella*. Thirty-three were killed. For each one of them, the Nazis decided to round up ten Italian men—"anyone they could find they just plucked off the street or some prisoners they already had in jail. Resistance members, of course, and Jews—only seventy-five Jews, as I mentioned before, but a high enough percentage—just civilians, some doctors, shopkeepers, a music teacher, regular people. A fourteen-year-old boy. A seventy-four-year-old man. An aristocrat.

The goal was three hundred and thirty, but you know the Nazis were over-achievers at killing; they managed to select an extra five."

Simon asked, "And, Jacobo, your uncle? You think he was in the Resistance, right?"

"Only after this, when we learned he had been killed, did my mother admit she knew. Her brother."

The first few underground spaces contained a couple of museum-like displays with photographs and memorabilia. We didn't have to hear about what happened in the inner sanctum where the massacre occurred to feel its horror. Into this space—dark, dank, claustrophobic—the victims were systematically led toward death.

"Of course, you see in here it is hardly big enough to kill three hundred thirty-five men all at once," Jacobo said. "So, what they did, the Nazis, was bring them in in groups of fives, hands tied behind their backs, and push them to kneel, so they could be shot straight into the head using only one bullet each. These were officers doing the shooting. Obviously, there wasn't a lot of room for the dead bodies and each of the next victims. You can only imagine how it was for the later ones to be forced to kneel down and die right on top of the bodies of those shot earlier."

"Officers personally carried this out?" said Simon.

"They were SS. Their operation. It was supposed to be covered up, which may have been one reason why they shot even the extra five, so no one would live to report on this. Not that an extra five dead Italians would have made any difference to them. It was said that one of the officers brought in a case of cognac to help calm their nerves. Apparently, that didn't prevent them from finishing the job with precision. And then they sealed the cave and set dynamite charges to bring the whole place down to bury the bodies."

"Grizzly. Sick," I said, envisioning the piles of bodies, the blood that must have splattered everywhere, the Nazis running away to escape being blown up. "How long did it take before news of what happened here eventually got out?"

"A few months later, after Rome was liberated by the Allies," Jacobo said. "There were rumors. Maybe someone had heard the explosions. Maybe someone had followed the trucks or seen them unloading. I don't know. But they started to dig through the place and found the bodies. What was left of them. The truth was discovered. The decision to make this a memorial came very soon after. Come, let's move on to the mausoleum. The sacred burial place."

In the cavernous hall three hundred thirty-five granite coffin lids lined up row after row, each with an engraved laurel wreath encircling the photograph, name, age at death, and profession of the victim. Suspended over it all was a giant concrete slab, an enormous hovering grave cover never to be lowered. Never forget.

In the middle of the third row back, Jacobo stopped and bowed his head, his lips whispering the kaddish prayer. Zosia took his arm. We stayed respectfully at his side but close enough to read the inscription. His uncle. The photo revealed a handsome guy with slight mustache. The inscription said twenty-nine years old. A chemist.

Jacobo said, "Amen," and turned to us. " He was the baby in my mother's family. Brilliant, already a university professor before the war when he was only 23."

"Was he married? Children?" I asked.

"No, he had a fiancée. She was also in the Resistance. She got through the war and married an American soldier. Lives in the US now. Chicago," Jacobo said. "Come, soon it will be dark. Let's move on before the worst of the rush hour."

As we walked back to the parking lot, I asked about the perpetrators of the *Fosse* Ardeatine massacre.

"Ironic you should ask now," Jacobo said. "One of the officers in charge, Ernst Priebke, has just been extradited back to Italy to stand trial."

"Now? After all these years," said Simon. "Extradited from where?"

"From Argentina. Priebke was in a British prison camp after the war waiting to stand trial but he escaped. He lived with a family in the

Tyrol for a while, then made his way to Argentina with a new baptism and a new identity."

"A new baptism? I don't understand," I said.

"That was part of the Vatican ratline operation. It legitimized getting new identity papers that could lead to passage out of Europe to welcoming Catholic countries like Argentina and Paraguay."

"Ah, the Vatican ratline," I said. "That must have been what helped the Nazi Rudolf Bucholz, a German I had occasion to meet both as a child and five years ago. He was sheltered in a monastery in northern Italy when Zionist compatriots of someone else I knew picked him up for transit. In fact, the priests up there were helping him store war planes and equipment he had confiscated and later used to barter his way to a new identity and life."

Zosia looked puzzled. "What? A Nazi got a new life by giving equipment to the Zionists? I don't understand. Where did he go?"

"Palestine on a ship. You know what Bricha was, I assume."

Zosia nodded. "Yes, I was supposed to go that way, too. Before I met Jacobo."

"Instead of getting a new baptism, this Nazi got a circumcision," said Simon. "That was the price he paid. The only price until five years ago."

"So, his new identity was as a Jew?" Jacobo shook his head in disbelief. "And he lived on in Israel?"

"He did. Until Lily herself unmasked him," said Simon. "We call her 'the Jewish Miss Marple.'"

Both of the Basevis looked puzzled.

"Agatha Christie," I said, "a British mystery writer, created a character called Jane Marple. An amateur detective pursuing cases in the area of her small village. There have been films, as well as the books. A cousin of mine is an avid Agatha Christie reader and has given me this nickname since I went looking for an antique Seder plate this particular Nazi stole from my family's apartment in Vienna and detained my father, whom we never saw again. Bucholz later committed far more heinous war crimes than looting art and possessions. When I found him, he was the owner of a prominent art gallery in Tel Aviv. Now he's in prison in Israel."

"That's a story worthy of Agatha Christie, indeed," said Zosia. "We have seen films with her other detective, the man Poirot, but not Miss Marple. We shall have to look for them."

"Just so you know," said Simon, "the actress in the films looks nothing like Lily. Thank goodness."

Nestled back in the car, I asked Jacobo more about his background. "Where were you and your parents when all this was happening? The war? The massacre?"

"In Switzerland. We, indeed, were lucky. My father was a partner in a small investment group with people he knew in Zurich, where he went to university. Gentile people. He ran the Rome office before the war. Mussolini was friendly to Jews—he did business with this company, even—until Hitler told him not to be. Yes, we had anti-Jewish laws as early as 1938, but life was good until the Nazis came to stay. My father traveled freely to and from Zurich. His partners told him in 1942 that Hitler was upset about Mussolini being too nice to the Jews. So, we left. Just like that. My parents, my two sisters, me. Five of us. Very lucky. My parents stayed in Zurich until they died. I am the only one who returned here to live; my sisters both married survivors, and they and their families live in Israel."

"And how did you and Zosia meet?"

She turned around to answer.

"I came to Rome with a group of young Zionist survivors in 1946. We all intended to move on to Palestine through Bricha, as I said. But there was a wait. I looked around, met some university students here, discovered I loved art, and worried that life in Israel would be a struggle I didn't think I could handle, after going through Auschwitz and losing my family. I suppose that sounds vain and shallow, doesn't it?"

"Oh, my goodness, not at all," I said. "I was fifteen when the war ended and I found out my parents were gone. I was living with an aunt and uncle in London and, once the initial shock wore off, I wanted nothing more than to forget about it all, enjoy life, go to parties. Of course, even after the war life was so austere, compared to now or even ten years later. But being young we didn't care or even realize it so much."

"That's true. Rome, like London, was badly damaged, but it was heaven after Poland, the ghetto, the camp," she said. "And Jacobo had returned. We both studied at the university. It's how we met. We got married in 1948 and we did go to live in Israel for a while after the War of Independence. But we were not kibbutzniks, so we returned here. We love Israel, though, and we have a place in Tel Aviv."

"We both have homes in Israel," said Simon. "Lily has a flat in Jerusalem and I have a home in Herzlia Pituach. In fact, we were in Israel just before we came to Rome."

By this time we were turning into the Excelsior driveway.

"We have so much in common," said Jacobo. "I'm delighted we have met. It has been a pleasure spending the afternoon with you."

"Thank you so much for taking us to the caves," I said. "Why don't you come into the hotel and have a drink with us? If you have time. I feel we could talk on and on."

"That would be wonderful," said Zosia. "We can do that. And I, too, think we have much in common and could fill more time with conversation."

Jacobo handed off his car keys to the hotel valet, and we all went into the lobby bar and ordered drinks. As we sat down, the concierge came over to Simon and handed him a bulky envelope.

"Ah, Signor Rieger, welcome back. A fax has arrived for you," he said, bowing slightly.

Simon thanked him, pulled out a tip, and tucked the envelope into the pocket of his sport coat.

When the drinks came, Jacobo lifted his whisky and toasted "*salute*," and Zosia led the "*l'chaim*" that followed.

"Lily, I love that you're also a vodka drinker. Must be our Polish Galitzianer roots."

"Perhaps. But my father was so ashamed of his background that I don't feel I have the right to claim them. Once he left home and moved to Vienna for medical training and the rest of his life, he shunned anything that reminded him of their Yiddish speaking or their more religious observance. I only met my grandparents and aunts and uncles and cousins in Lwów once when I was just six years old. From how my father talked, I had pictured them as living in some hovel wearing rags and begging. The truth was they lived in apartments maybe not as big as ours in Vienna, but nice. They seemed to me to be not so different from my other grandparents, except they were much warmer and more affectionate. Yes, they spoke some Yiddish, but also German, like we did, and Polish."

"Did any of them survive the war?"

"The grandparents died within the next two years—before the war started. That I knew. As for the others, I don't think so. At least, I've never heard from any of them. But it's also possible no one on that side of the family would have known how to find me. That's why it's such a coincidence we have met and we're discussing this. Right now I'm grappling with this question after so many years of not even thinking about them, as if they never existed. Which in a way, for me, was the reality."

"What do you mean? Why now?"

"It's complicated."

I looked over to Simon as if to check how much to reveal. But he and Jacobo were deep in conversation about Israeli politics, a topic guaranteed to engage two Jews even slightly concerned about that country. I could handle this without his guidance

"Through a very complicated set of circumstances that I'm not at liberty to completely explain, here in Rome I saw a painting that I believe was my grandparents' in Lwów. My aunt and uncle had a gallery, I think I remember, and gave this as a gift for the grandparents' fiftieth anniversary. That is why my parents and I were in Lwów the one and only time in my life. The artist's name was A. Kozakiewicz; it's inscribed on a plate on the gilded frame of the painting, just as the one for my grandparents was. Do you know about this artist? Was he famous?"

"Yes, Antoni Kozakiewicz. He painted in the realist genre. One of his most famous paintings is called 'Praying Jews.' It was reproduced all over Poland, and many Jews owned copies. He also painted gypsy families, peasants, village markets. Home-style is one way to put it in English."

"Bourgeois is how my father described the painting. Not in a flattering way. Simon said the same thing. How do you know so much about Kozakiewicz? You left Poland so young."

"Yes," Zosia said, "but as I told you I developed an interest in art when I was in university. Not much in Polish art, of course, but I wouldn't demean someone like Kozakiewicz as bourgeois. He was a product of his time and place. It was a style. And the subject matter was there in front of them. I did learn about Maurycy Gottlieb when I took a seminar in Tel Aviv several years ago. Kozakiewicz was briefly discussed because he painted Orthodox Jews praying in a synagogue on Yom Kippur. As did Gottlieb. Two different paintings with the same title, two different painters, one Jewish and one not."

"So A. Kozakiewicz wasn't Jewish?"

"No. But his painting is very sensitive and respectful. So, perhaps he didn't suffer from the hereditary Polish disease of anti-Semitism. I'm surprised, if you remember so little about your father's family, you remember a painting they had. You said you were—what?—six when you met them."

"Because of my father's very vocal criticism of the painting the celebration erupted into a huge family fight. His brothers, who still lived in Lwów, lit into him for his snobbishness and estrangement from the family, his ingratitude for their support—and that of the grandparents—of his studies. Things I didn't know about and I doubt my mother did either."

"I am sorry," Zosia said. "It seems there are always disputes in families, but it's a shame this is the primary memory you have."

"My mother tried to shush up my father and save the day. She pushed me off to play with the one girl cousin, who I think was a little older than I was, and her older brother, who wanted nothing to do with either of us silly girls, of course. The other girl was okay. She was blonde. I don't even remember her name."

Now Zosia took my hand. "I'm sorry. I don't remember many people from Lwów, but what was your family name?"

"Weinberg. Not exactly unique."

"No, you're right, and I don't recall anyone named Weinberg. But where did you see this painting so recently?"

"Here in Rome. In a restaurant in Vatican City."

"The Vatican? Were you visiting the museum? I know one of the curators. He does an amazing private tour."

"No, Simon had something to attend to there."

At that moment there must have been in a lull in the mens' conversation, as Simon turned at the mention of his name. I wondered if I had said too much.

"I've just been telling Jacobo," he said, "about where we were before we met him in the ghetto yesterday. And about our trip back to the Vatican this morning. I was just asking him if there might have been involvement by Ukrainians in the ratline? Ukrainian priests, for instance."

"I can't be sure, but probably," said Jacobo. "There were certainly Nazi sympathizers among priests with power in the Vatican hierarchy. One, Alois Hudal, was Austrian and secretly a Nazi and undercover informer for the Germans. There were Vatican rescue committees in various countries liberated by the Russians that supposedly got Nazis out before the true crackdown of the Iron Curtain. German Nazis and Nazis native to those places. Which there were plenty of in every country."

"How do you know this?" Simon asked.

"A career dealing with property in Rome has educated me in many ways. Some knowledge of Swiss banking history has also been very instructive on such aspects of history," said Jacobo.

"Lily was telling me she has just found what she thinks is a remnant of her family's history in Lwów. You know, we should say Lviv now. For me it will always be Lwów, and when the Nazis came it was Lemberg again," said Zosia. "Are you going to pursue this thread?"

"I don't know. I don't care about the painting. It was just a shock to see it again. If, indeed, it was the original. Was Kozakiewicz the type of artist who might have been reproduced?"

"The Jews at prayer painting I'm sure has been reproduced a lot, like Gottlieb's, probably by Jews," she said. "A random scene like the one you describe—I doubt it. Especially with a gold frame. And you said your aunt and uncle owned a gallery business."

"I think so. It may have been that the aunt's family owned one in Warsaw, and they had a branch in Lwów. I know one of the aunts was from Warsaw."

"My parents had friends named Berkowski who owned a business that had some paintings but mostly Jewish objects. Seder plates, Kiddush cups, menorahs for Chanukah, candlesticks, spice boxes. It was a very large shop. I don't know that I would call it a gallery, but there may have been some pictures there. And they could order other types of art."

"Berkowski. I don't know that name," I said. "I was close to a man—really a surrogate uncle to me—who was a major collector in Warsaw before the war. Art, including Gottlieb and even Impressionist painters, but also Judaica. He probably knew that business. He could have been a client. He had given my family the antique Seder plate that led me to stumble upon the Nazi-turned-Israeli. He only died a few years ago, just after I recovered the plate."

"Lily and her cousin, who's a Judaica expert, run a foundation dedicated to helping people find art and other valuable possessions looted by the Nazis. It's based in Jerusalem," said Simon.

"Wonderful work," said Zosia. "So, back to my question. Now that you've seen your grandparents painting again, are you going to pursue where it's been all this time and find out if any of your family in Lwów survived? How did the restaurant in Rome get it?"

"Someone from Lviv brought it to the restaurant and apparently took it back. But, yes," I said, "I've just decided to pursue what happened to my family there. My conversation with you has convinced me it's the right thing to do. No, more than that, it's what I want to do. Simon, I want to go to Lviv. Are you in?"

He reached for my hand and held it. "Of course."

"Good for you," said Zosia. "I myself have not been back and will not go. I know plenty about my family. No one I ever met or heard of in my childhood survived. I hope you don't find that to be the case. But I think you've made the right decision. Keep me posted on your trip and what you find out."

She looked at her watch. "Jacobo, the time. We must go. The performance starts in forty-five minutes."

"What are you seeing?"

"Shakespeare's 'Merchant of Venice.' We would ask you to join us but we're invited to the box of friends."

"And the performance is in Italian," said Simon. "I know the play but I think it would be frustrating for me in Italian."

"Good point," said Jacobo. "Though I'd gladly forfeit my ticket. Shakespeare is not really, as you'd say, my thing."

We bade them farewell and went back to our room. Simon took the envelope out of his pocket. Several sheets of paper, stapled together, emerged. He quickly scanned one and separated the last two from the sheaf.

"Here," he said, putting his arm around me as he handed them to me. "These are for you."

My first glance showed a list of names, each followed by two columns of dates. All the surnames were Weinberg. All the dates down the second column were from 1939 to 1945.

"What is this?"

"I asked Avi to see if someone from headquarters could get a list from Yad Vashem of known victims from Lwów/Lemberg/Lviv, whatever. Victims named Weinberg."

I could barely see the paper as tears quickly blurred my vision and dripped onto it. Because I was so overcome with emotion for this man holding me and now getting out his handkerchief.

"Thank you," I said. "I guess."

"Yes, let's be careful what we wish for. I don't want this to unduly upset you."

"I'm going in eyes wide open with no expectations. I think it's important to find out what happened but I'm still not as invested in this as I was for the Seder plate. In fact, it's been such a day— between Father Stash dying, Franco's tale of woe, the trip with Zosia and Jacobo . . ."

"And almost being run over by a car, don't forget that."

"Yes. All connected, maybe? But what I was going to say is that I'm not even going to study the Yad Vashem list right now tonight. I'll have time on the flights. And I didn't even ask you about the other pages of the fax."

"A message from Avi specifically assigning me to go to Lviv to look for the codex. Obviously, it's looted. It's the first lead in the trail of archives that disappeared from the Golden Rose synagogue that was destroyed in the war. It was a famous place, and the scholar The TaZ was one of its early rabbis. In fact, this is one of the first pieces at all of anything that's turned up from that part of Ukraine."

"It's amazing to me that the Soviet Union has been broken up for five years and the foundation has not had one claim. I guess the government of Israel hasn't either," I said. "Until the Israel Museum was asked to buy this manuscript."

"By The Duck, whoever he is," said Simon. "Maybe we will make him quack."

"Very funny. Or fly away. Again."

Chapter 6

Other than the fight between my father and his brothers, my primary memory of my prior trip to this city was of how surprisingly warm and loving my grandparents were, even though they were meeting me for the first time. In Vienna my Heilbrun grandparents, whom I saw several times a week, were pleasant to me, and obviously caring, but stiff. My grandfather, a prominent surgeon at the equally prominent university hospital, was very busy and self-important; Grandmama was simply self-absorbed, mainly about her wardrobe and hairdo. Yes, she was concerned about people. Certain people whom she considered worthy of knowing. What they thought of her and her family. And when and where she could socialize with them. My mother and her twin brother Erich could have cared less about any of this. The same was true of their older sibling, my Aunt Charlotte, who was happy to live her married life in London, away from her mother. This was especially fortunate for me when she became my second mother after the kindertransport.

My arrogant father could have been my maternal grandparents' son, instead of their son-in-law. In the end, to Hitler all the Jews were the same: the snobs who thought they were aristocrats, the bourgeoisie who bought "home-style" art, the impoverished religious scholars, grandparents, parents, children, the young, the old.

Since the war I had been back to Vienna, once, and I had gone to Warsaw for that conference with Arthur. But Lviv seemed older and colder and less friendly than anywhere I had ever been in Europe. It was night in December, which didn't help either. No doubt I only imagined that the first locals we encountered—the cab driver, hotel clerk, concierge, bellman, bartender—looked at us thinking dirty Jews. Maybe just because we weren't locals? Lviv, formerly Lwów and Lemberg, had seen its share of foreigners: invaders who trampled through toward perceived greater prizes east or west, staying long enough to rule for a while and loot and slaughter. In their wake they always left refugees escaping the tsunami of one oppressor or another. The actual Ukrainians were now enjoying a rare period of self-rule. Or enduring it.

We checked into the vintage George Hotel, a multi-neo edifice— neo-Baroque, neo-Renaissance—dating from 1901. The oldest continuously operated and most storied and historically elegant lodging in the city. The lobby and public areas retained some of its former glory; the rooms were purely mid-century Soviet in furnishing and operation. Presumably, the place had suffered during the war and had been renovated since 1936, but the imposing marble staircase in the lobby reminded me I had stayed there with my parents. If it were indeed the top hotel in the thirties, my father would have stayed nowhere else. Did that aggravate his brothers, too?

His brothers. My family in Lviv. What was I doing here? Where would I start?

Traveling from Rome to Lviv that day, I pored over the list of murdered Lwów/Lemberg/Lviv Weinbergs from the Yad Vashem Central Database of Shoah Victims' Names Simon had given me the night before. Really straining to remember the relatives in the room at the restaurant where my grandparents' party was and the next day at their house, I thought a few names rang a bell: Chaim (three of them listed), Nathan (only one), Esther (five), Shlomo (two). I narrowed down by ages. One Chaim and the Nathan could have been my uncles, two Esthers an aunt and one Shlomo my boy cousin. There was a common source for the listing of several Weinbergs: one Chaim, Nathan, one Esther, Shlomo. The name of the source was one Freya Weinberg Zusman (née Rubin) of Nahariya, Israel, who added Pages of Testimony in 1959. Freya. That might have been the name of one of the aunts. But Zusman? Did she remarry after the war?

I asked Simon to ask for another favor from his Mossad colleague and "master," Avi Ben Ze'ev: Could he find out if this woman was still alive in Israel? Simon called Avi from the Vienna airport while we snacked during a three-hour layover between flights. Before we boarded the next plane, Avi called back with an answer. Freya Weinberg Zusman had died in 1992. Mr. Israel Zusman, her husband, had died in 1982. There was no record of any surviving children for either of them. Dead end. Literally. Still, Freya was the only lead, the only survivor, if I even remembered her name correctly, of the family here I met once. Could I ask Avi for one more favor? Could he send me her actual Pages of Testimony?

"Anything for Lily," I heard his loud but boisterous voice transcend the cell phone from Simon's ear. "My favorite Nazi hunter."

By the time we arrived in Lviv it was eight-thirty in the evening. We had a nightcap in the bar, neither hungry nor energetic enough to bother with dinner. Upstairs, I lay down on the bed clutching the list and rereading the names I had circled during the day. Another clue popped up.

"Berkowski."

"What?" Simon came out of the bathroom drying his hands.

"Berkowski. Didn't Zosia say her parents knew Judaica dealers in Warsaw named Berkowski?"

"Yes, I guess so," he said. "Why?"

"One of the Esthers. Esther Weinberg, née Berkowski. Born 1902, Warsaw, died 1941, Lwów ghetto. Husband Chaim, born 1899, Lemberg, died 1941, USSR . . .

"Wait! Oh, my God. I can connect a whole chain: Mother of Shlomo, born 1924, Lwów, died 1941 question mark, USSR; Chaim brother of Nathan, born 1897, died Bergen-Belsen 1943. Husband of Freya Zusman, Freya who submitted all the information. Simon, I think this is my family. If this is the right Esther. Names are coming back to me. I think Shlomo was the name of the boy cousin. So, he would have been twelve when I met him. But the girl. He had a sister. There's no sister mentioned, or daughter of Chaim and Esther. The other aunt and uncle had no children, I recall. Freya and Nathan, they would have been. Can we call Zosia on Jacobo's mobile? Maybe she knows more about the Berkowski family. If any of them survived, maybe another lead?"

Simon dialed Jacobo. Momentarily, I was on the line with Zosia.

"Zosia, Simon got Yad Vashem records faxed to him. I just discovered an Esther Berkowski Weinberg, born in Warsaw, who died in Lwów. Do you think she's possibly from the family you knew who were Judaica dealers? Maybe she was my aunt."

"Oh, Lily, how exciting that you've found a clue," she said. "I honestly don't remember any of the Berkowskis myself. I have blocked much of my memory. It's the only way to have survived. Thank God for Jacobo and my children and grandchildren. They all save me from my past. It's a cliché, I know, but I always tell them, life is for the living. I don't need to remember more. My wrist and my legs remind me every day. I, too, sent the forms for my family to Yad Vashem. A long time ago I searched the list for any other names I might have remembered. They were all on it. No need to look for anyone else."

"I understand. I've never looked for my father's family before. I had so little contact with them. My aunt in London registered my mother's side, including my father, but I was too young and even then didn't really remember the names of my father's relatives. I kind of forgot about them to be honest. Knowing the truth now, if I've got the names right, tells me they're mostly gone. Except I can't find any information about the girl cousin I played with. Either she survived or the aunt who recorded the rest didn't know what happened to her. Do you have any ideas about that?"

"Maybe she was hidden," Zosia said.

"Oh. I never thought about that. But after the war wouldn't she have looked for her family?"

"Who knows? It was all so complicated, wasn't it? Good night, Lily." She clicked off.

Still holding the phone I said to Simon, "Just like that . . . tada, good night. Well, it is late. And she's not keen on dredging up the past."

"Did Zosia remember anything about the Judaica dealers and their family."

"No. But she did give me something new to think about."

"What?"

"Zosia said the missing girl cousin might have been hidden."

"Interesting. Of course, it only adds more mystery to the mystery and, I'm afraid, more difficulty in turning up any information."

PART II

Lwów/Lviv/Lemberg,
Poland/Soviet- and German-occupied, Ukraine,
German-occupied, Ukraine 1936 to 1948

Chapter 7

Chanah hated it when people commented on her blonde hair. Jews, around whom she spent most of her time, after all, said she looked like a little *shikseh,* a non-Jewish girl. The few non-Jews she encountered when she was with her mother or father—on the trolley, in parks or in the shops—said things like "where did this one come from?" This was especially true in her parents' shop, where gentiles would come only to peruse a small selection of Polish art interspersed among the Jewish ritual items and rare Hebrew books. Chanah was happy and proud to be Jewish. She loved the holidays. She loved her Yiddish-speaking grandparents. She loved studying about Jewish history and learning some Hebrew. As much as would be taught to a girl in an Orthodox school.

Her mother told her there were other blondes on the Berkowski side of the family and showed her photographs of her sandy-haired brother, for whom Shlomo was named, who had died in the Great War. That did nothing to alleviate Chanah's distress; a boy, she reasoned, would not have been teased.

"You're wrong," her mother said. "The old *bubbes* called him a *shaigetz,* a gentile boy, and he didn't like it either. Although it probably helped him survive the day-to-day life in the army. As long as no one was watching when he changed his underwear."

Chanah didn't understand what this meant until about the age of ten, when she got up the courage to ask Esther. The explanation helped her feel better about being a Jewish girl, as compared to a Jewish boy.

Lwów could often be dreary. The winters were long and cold. In the Weinberg family and milieu, time and seasons were marked by the Jewish holidays. An early and unusually warm Rosh Hashanah would be viewed as the year "we had a long summer." A cold, rainy Pesach would be the "year winter didn't end." The palette ranged from grey to black most of the time. The air felt either dank or brutally freezing. Which made summer sunshine, eight hours of it at the peak of a perfect July day, feel like deliverance from above. So a celebration in the winter was like a light in a tunnel.

When her aunt and uncle from Vienna were planning to come to Lwów with their daughter, her cousin Lily, for the grandparents' fiftieth wedding anniversary, Chanah pestered her mother with questions.

"When was the last time they came to Lwów?" *Never.*

"Why do Papa and Uncle Nathan have a bet they will not really come?" *Experience.*

"What is Aunt Elisabeth like?" *I don't know, I never met her.*

"Why do Papa and Uncle Nathan get mad when they talk about Uncle Yankel? *A long story about grownup matters a long time ago.*

"Lily is two years younger than me. Do I have to talk to her and play with her?" *Yes, it's only for a short time. The night of the party will be hectic at the restaurant. And the next day we will go to Bubbe and Zayde's for lunch. Then they will leave and go back to Vienna.*

As the occasion approached, Esther took Chanah out shopping for a new dress, deep blue velvet on top with a brocaded taffeta skirt. The same day Chaim took Shlomo, who had grown to almost the height of his father, for his first real man's suit to be made by Shlemberg the Tailor. Esther's dark green wool dress with beaded collar was the most expensive she had ever bought, she told Chanah.

"Papa told me to buy whatever we want," she said. "Your Aunt Elisabeth from Vienna will be very fashionable. We don't want them to think we're the country bumpkin relatives."

"What's a bumpkin?"

Esther laughed. "A person whom other people that think they know everything would consider to be without good taste in clothes or good manners."

"Like the people in the picture you're giving Bubbe and Zayde?"

"Those people are peasants and they actually live in the countryside, where they grow the food we eat and might have lovely manners. It's just an expression snobbish people might use about people they don't think are as good as they are."

"And Papa says Uncle Yankel is a snob. Does that mean Aunt Elisabeth and Lily are, too?"

"Not necessarily. We will see."

When the night of the anniversary party arrived, Chanah and Shlomo were enlisted to help their parents steer their way into the restaurant while maneuvering the giant painting that was the gift into the private dining room. It was heavy, and it was all they could do to avoid hitting a wall in the narrow corridor from the entrance. As it was, people sitting in the main part of the restaurant stopped eating and wondered what was being moved. Several got up from their tables and followed the procession into the room, watching while the ribbon and paper were removed.

Bubbe shrieked with delight and wiped tears from her face when the painting was uncovered. She had seen it, and loved it, at the flagship Berkowski shop in Warsaw when they all went there to celebrate the fiftieth anniversary of Esther's parents after Yom Kippur.

"Oh, look, Yossel, and what a gorgeous frame they put on it. Gold. With the artist's name: A. Kozakiewicz. So elegant," Bubbe said to her husband.

Zayde was less impressed—"who needs art?"—but the sight of his wife so excited made him happy. He hugged and kissed her, something Chanah had never seen before, and shouted a big thank you.

Chanah looked around the room and knew everyone in it— elderly great-aunts and uncles, a few close friends and neighbors of her grandparents—except the three people standing behind the main table. There had not been time for formal introductions. What she saw was an elegantly dressed woman, wearing a dark red dress very similar to Esther's, and a man in a black suit who looked just like her Uncle Nathan, except thinner. Next to them was a girl younger than her in a bright red dress, also velvet, with a white lace collar that Chanah thought was a little babyish. The girl's hair was dark and curly. So these were her relatives from Vienna: Aunt Elisabeth, Uncle Yankel, and Cousin Lily.

If her uncle thought no one could hear his murmured criticism of the painting to his wife, he was wrong. Chanah heard the words "bourgeois" and "peasants," and her aunt telling him to shush. But it was too late. The "grownup matters" all spilled out for everyone to hear. Chanah had certainly never known anything about why Papa and Uncle Nathan were haranguing their brother—his ingratitude for their hard work, and that of the grandparents, to put him through school. When the yelling stopped, Uncle Yankel walked out of the dining room. Bubbe's tears of joy had turned to sobs of anguish. Zayde stood next to her, scowling at all his three sons but powerless to do anything about the commotion.

This was the moment Chanah and Lily were separately directed by their respective mothers to sit down and talk to each other and literally plunked onto chairs next to Shlomo, who was sorting trading cards with pictures of trains and ships and oblivious to the fracas.

Aunt Elisabeth had brought gifts for Chanah and Shlomo that she presented now. Chanah got a book about children living on a kibbutz in Palestine. Shlomo got one about Dr. Albert Einstein's days as a student in Berlin. And Lily's mother had brought her own daughter a new book, too, about a woman in America called Betsy Ross. So they all had something to keep them busy. Lily wanted to read her book to Chanah and Shlomo.

"Okay," said Chanah, indulging her younger cousin's apparent desire to show off.

Lily read well, finished about three pages, and then said, "Why don't you two read from your books, too? Let's take turns."

They agreed to do that until dinner would come. The eruption among the Weinberg brothers had delayed the signal, to come from Aunt Freya, for the waiters to serve. When Shlomo started to read, Lily stood up, said "Excuse me for a moment," and went to talk to her mother. Her father had not returned to the dining room. Bubbe and Zayde were seated at their places in the center of the main table holding hands quietly. Elisabeth and her sisters-in-law were sitting in a corner of the room.

Chanah heard Lily ask if her papa was going to come back.

"I don't know, sweetheart, but we will stay and have a nice time. It is your grandparents' anniversary, after all. And you're finally meeting your cousins."

"Yes, but . . ."

"Go back to the table, Lily. Please. Now."

Chanah hadn't seen her father and Uncle Nathan leave so was surprised when they walked back into the room with their arms around Uncle Yankel. He was carrying a glass half-filled with whisky, and his tie had been loosened. No one said anything as the Weinberg brothers quickly settled down in their seats at the table. Aunt Freya went to tell the restaurant staff to start serving.

The rest of the evening there were people getting up to say nice things about Bubbe and Zayde. Even Uncle Yankel and Aunt Elisabeth, who gave their gift of a glass vase.

The next day they went to the grandparents for lunch. Bubbe had been cooking the lunch all week, standing way too much on her perpetually swollen legs and feet, a fact Zayde mentioned to everyone as they helped themselves to the dairy feast of pickled trout and three different varieties of herring, deep-fried gefilte fish balls, both sweet and savory noodle kugels, cheese blintzes, egg salad, warm homemade apple sauce, fresh bread and rolls, and desserts ranging from cinnamon kuchen to chocolate cake to crispy sugar cookies.

"Goodness, look at this," Elisabeth said. "She made it all herself?"

Her sisters-in-law assumed correctly their peer from Vienna did not do her own cooking.

"We offered to help or even to have it catered," said Aunt Freya to Elisabeth. "But Mama wouldn't hear of it."

None of the great-aunts or uncles or friends were there, just the immediate family, a group of eleven squeezed around a dining room table meant for eight at the most. There was not enough room for Chanah and Lily to have chairs, so they each straddled on the adjacent laps of their parents. This arrangement was hardly ideal, but it offered a moment of fraternal bonding for Chanah's Papa and Uncle Yankel, who exchanged eye rolls as they and their wives adjusted their not-so-tiny daughters on their thighs. The girls were not any happier to be treated like babies. However, they were served first and ate as fast as possible before sliding down off their relieved parents.

Bubbe told them to go into the spare bedroom, where they found two wrapped boxes, each marked with one of their names and containing a doll to play with. Lily named hers Greta, and Chanah called hers Rosa.

"Like the Golden Rosa," she told her cousin.

"Who was that?"

"A very famous and brave woman. She saved the synagogue from being taken away from the Jews."

"I don't understand," said Lily. "How did she do that? Where? What synagogue?"

"Here in Lwów. We have a beautiful synagogue called the Golden Rose after her. Her family built it, but some bad people wanted the building and the land back. She went to talk to them, and the Jews kept the synagogue."

"What was so brave about that?"

"They were bad people, and they didn't let her go back to her family. They never saw her again. So, the story turned out to be sad for her, even though she saved the synagogue."

"I don't think she was brave. I think she was stupid to go. Or her family was bad to let her go," said Lily.

"I never thought of it that way, but you may be right. You're pretty smart for a little kid," said Chanah. "But the synagogue is beautiful. If you could stay here longer, we could take you to see it."

"We go to synagogue, too," said Lily, "but only once or twice a year."

"We're pretty much the same. But Zayde goes every week. To the *alte shul,* it's Orthodox. We go to the Temple. It's Reform. Mama says it's the modern way, even though my school is Orthodox."

Shlomo joined them and opened his gift, a jigsaw puzzle depicting a map of Paris. Soon, the dolls were abandoned, and all three sat on the floor engrossed in fitting the pieces together.

The adults were also on their best behavior. Though the notorious painting had assumed a spot of honor over the sofa in the grandparents' front room, it was no longer a topic of discussion. A poster of the Holy Land that had hung there before sat propped against the single bed in the room where the grandchildren played. When the grownups finished lunch, Bubbe insisted that photos be taken of her and Zayde with family members sitting with them on the sofa under the picture. Uncle Yankel sulked but complied with his mother's wish to be photographed solely with his parents and then along with Elisabeth and Lily, the latter on Zayde's lap.

"Who knows when this will ever happen again?"

When Bubbe said this, she was likely only thinking about her and Zayde's old age. She was not political. In fact, that weekend in December 1936 none of the Weinberg family spoke directly about what terror Hitler was already wreaking on the Jews in Germany. The sisters-in-law, though, found a common topic of conversation in that week's abdication of King Edward VIII. Aunt Freya was vociferous.

"She's a *nafkeh,* that Mrs. Simpson. That means a tramp or slut, Elisabeth."

"I know. Thanks. He's not such a prize either," said her presumably

73

more assimilated sister-in-law from Vienna. "And friendly to Hitler, I think. The British are better off without him."

"Shhh," said Esther, "not in front of the *kinder*. Nothing about Hitler."

Chanah, all of ten years old but an avid radio listener, added her girlish take.

"I think it's romantic," she said. "Giving up the throne for love."

"Youth," said Bubbe, "innocence. As if it were all that simple."

No one knew what she meant or wanted to ask. However, if Bubbe said it, it was to be taken as gospel in the Weinberg family.

Soon the visitors from Vienna got up to catch their train.

"I want to stay longer," said Lily. "It's so nice here, and I like Chanah."

"Maybe we will come back, or Chanah will come to visit us. Would you like that? Chanah, what do you think?"

Chanah looked at her parents. "Maybe," her mother said.

The Weinberg brothers said nothing. The prodigal from Vienna was leaving. The family reunion had been contentious but ended with at least a truce. The brothers shook hands silently, the sisters-in-law hugged. Bubbe cried when her youngest son gave her a peck on the cheek and lifted up Lily for her grandma to hug. Zayde opened his arms wide to give the family a joint bear hug and gently patted the top of Lily's head. Elisabeth juggled her handbag and the box of Bubbe's baked goodies pressed on her for the train ride as her husband walked out, hands-free, to the taxi that waited outside.

"Well, that's done. Now you've met them. I hope you're satisfied, Elisabeth, because that's happened this once, and it's never going to happen again."

"But I want to see Chanah again," said Lily. "We had fun. Even Shlomo is nice—for a boy."

Her father acted as if she had said nothing. Her mother tenderly squeezed her shoulder, and the taxi bounced along on the cobblestone road. Jack spoke only once on the way to the station.

"When is this city ever going to enter the twentieth century and pave its damned streets?" Her father sure didn't like his hometown, thought Lily. No, we're never coming back here.

Chapter 8

Bubbe would never have called herself a prophet; the notion would have made her laugh. But she remembered her words—"Who knows when this will ever happen again?"—the afternoon fifteen months later when Nathan and Chaim came over to her house to tell her that, in the aftermath of Hitler marching into Austria a few days earlier, his henchmen had taken Yankel into custody. It was enough that Zayde had suffered a stroke during the night after an evening listening to the radio reports about troop movements from Germany and the resignation of Austria's Chancellor Kurt von Schuschnigg that was the ultimate capitulation leading to the invasion and takeover known as the Anschluss. Bubbe knew about what was happening in Vienna but was adamant that her local sons call their brother to tell them about Zayde's condition. Maybe her youngest could and would get on a train and travel one more time to Lwów to visit his fading father. Yankel was a brilliant doctor—he could help, talk with the doctors at the Jewish Hospital, give them advice on handling the case.

"At least he should know what's happening," she said before Chaim called Vienna, tacitly acknowledging the likelihood that Yankel, who until the anniversary celebration had not been home in twenty years, would choose not to come. Even without the Anschluss, which they knew would be the excuse, admittedly a good one.

Chanah and Shlomo heard their father speaking to Aunt Elisabeth on the telephone. From his responses they patched together the story before Chaim could even tell Esther, busy in the kitchen where running water prevented her from hearing.

"Elisabeth? Oh, my. Yes, we knew Hitler was there. But your father. Such a respected person and doctor. Yankel, I mean Jack, too. If any Jews were to be protected, I would have . . . no, I guess not. It doesn't matter to that monster. What? Your father on his knees . . . scrubbing the sidewalk. We will be fine. Yes, my father, well, he is comfortable. Thank you, thank you. I will tell her. Yes, give kisses to that little Lily."

He hung up the phone in their entry hall and went into the kitchen. Esther whispered, "*Nu*, so what did she say? It sounds like Yankel isn't coming to see your father."

Chanah and Shlomo appeared.

Chaim shook his head and said to his children, "You heard, right? Enough? So there's no point now to tell your mother in private."

They nodded.

"Tell me what? Chaim, what did she say?"

"Since Hitler came to Vienna, it's been bedlam. And even the rich and fancy Jews like Elisabeth and her family are affected. The Germans have lists. They came for Yankel last night. Took him away. An SS officer with a group of underlings. They took silverware, some fancy Seder plate they got from their friend in Warsaw, Nachman Tanski . . ."

"Tanski? He's one of my father's biggest clients. He's a Zionist leader. They know him?"

"Apparently. Anyway, she knows Yankel is detained right there in Vienna for now but will probably be sent to a place in Germany, Dachau, soon. A lot of Jewish men were rounded up. If she could get together the money to leave Austria, she could get him out and take Lily and go. Maybe to her sister in London. No doubt she can put together the money. But she won't leave her parents. And they won't go. They say it will blow over. Even now, after her father was beaten and forced to go down on his knees to wash the sidewalk and the steps of the university hospital where he has been so important all these years."

Esther sat down and put her hands over her eyes.

"*Oy, gevalt,*" she said. "Hitler. Such a *mamzer.*"

"What's a *mamzer?*" Chanah had never heard that word before.

"It's a really bad person," said Chaim, "a person who does a lot of bad things to good people."

"Are you going to tell all this to Bubbe? I don't think it's a good idea," said Shlomo. "With Zayde in the hospital and all."

"No, Shlomo, you're wrong," said Chanah, "Bubbe must know the truth. She can take it."

Esther and Chaim looked at each other as they listened to their daughter, just turned ten, discuss the toughness of her grandmother. Chanah is cut from the same cloth, thought Esther. I hope she never needs to prove it.

"I don't know," said Chaim. "I will call Nathan and see what he thinks."

"Do what you want, Papa, but Bubbe also can tell when someone isn't telling the truth. Like that time when I went over there with Shlomo and he . . ."

"Chanah!"

Her brother put his finger to his mouth to shut her up.

"Well, it wasn't that serious," said Chanah.

"You're a tattle tale, a little rat," he said.

Esther laughed and said, "We know what you're talking about. Bubbe told me when I came to get you. The cake she had baked for *shul* you ate half of and told her you didn't know who did it."

Shlomo blushed and nodded.

"Your bubbe loves you so much. You're right, Chanah, she doesn't like lying, but this one was pretty easy for her to figure out. And, you know Bubbe, she had another cake just like it ready to go into the oven. So no harm done, though it wasn't good to lie about it, Shlomo."

"But telling her about Uncle Yankel could damage her health," Chaim said. "That's a very different consequence than needing another cake for *shul.*"

"Well, ask Uncle Nathan," said Chanah. "I still think she can take it. I think she already knows Zayde is going to die. She has told me about living through pogroms and seeing her parents' store burn down and her baby sister die. Bubbe is tough."

In the short term Bubbe took the news about her youngest just as Chanah predicted. She carried on, went to the hospital every day to see Zayde through his final days, mourned him when the time came two weeks later. Chaim called Elisabeth again to tell her about Zayde. By that time Yankel/Jack was interned at Dachau.

Six months later, though, Chaim's fears became reality when his mother suffered a massive heart attack and died that night in the hospital after a neighbor had found her unconscious on the kitchen floor. Bubbe had insisted on staying in her apartment on her own, refused her sons' offers to move in with either of them. She had not just celebrated, but also hosted, the Passover Seders for everyone only a few weeks after Zayde's death; she had gone with them for a holiday in the mountains in the summer; and when she died was baking her special *lekach* for Rosh Hashanah, which was coming in three days. The neighbor had smelled two pans of burnt honey cake shriveled to ash before she found Bubbe on the floor pelted by spilled raisins. Wizened and dried up, like the simple woman lying on the floor departing on her own terms a family and existence soon to be extinguished by outside forces beyond their control.

For the Weinbergs of Lwów it was the saddest holiday ever. They all remembered her statement: "Who knows when this will ever happen again?"

Chapter 9

As 1938 drew to a close, Chanah's parents talked about the joyous milestones of the two years before—the fiftieth wedding celebrations of both sets of grandparents, the entire Weinberg family together one last time. They had only to look at the A. Kozakiewicz painting, hanging on their dining room wall since Bubbe's death, to remember how happy Bubbe and Zayde were to see their family reunited for what turned out to be the last time. Family gatherings were not only smaller and sadder but also more subdued. Their own losses weighed heavily enough, but there was the added burden of worrying about the world around them. When Chanah's father had made the call to Aunt Elisabeth to tell her about Bubbe's death in September, there had been no change in the news about Yankel/Jack; he was still in Dachau, as far as his wife knew. The existence of Jews in Vienna, even for assimilated self-proclaimed aristocrats Herr Doktor and Frau Heilbrun, was a breakneck downhill spiral of new restrictions and austerity almost on a daily basis. Elisabeth's twin brother Erich had been ready to go to Palestine the year before, she said, but her mother had had a slight stroke and he stayed home. Now he was threatening to go to Shanghai. Yet, Elisabeth's parents stuck to their intractable guns: the Nazis were a fad that would pass. It would be more difficult for them to emigrate as a family, even if her parents would consider it, since her husband had been interned for so long and communication from or about him was minimal. Plus, she admitted, she no longer had enough cash to pay the bribes and buy the tickets they would need to get away.

"If we can help, please don't hesitate to call me," Chaim had told his sister-in-law. Esther, listening with the children, nodded, which made Chanah very happy. "My parents didn't have much, but they did leave a little money to all of us, including to Yankel. We are about to wire it to you. I can add some from us, from Esther and myself, and I'm sure Nathan and Freya would contribute."

"I'm overwhelmed with gratitude," said Elisabeth. "The way Jack treated you all . . ."

"There's no need to be overwhelmed," Chaim said. "We are family. And we could all tell that you are a fine person, Elisabeth, and your Lily is a little doll. Yankel, well, I hope he has treated you well, because you deserve it. And I hope you saw, when you were here in Lwów, that we are not the bumpkins he might have told you we were."

Bumpkins again, thought Chanah. Why were her parents so worried about what Aunt Elisabeth thought of them? They always told her not to worry about what people said, like about her looking like a *shikseh* because of her blonde hair, but hadn't they noticed Elisabeth didn't seem anything like the same kind of snob her husband was?

"Thank you, Chaim," Elisabeth said. "The inheritance from your parents will be welcome and very much appreciated right now. We can use it for everyday expenses. Food is getting harder to get, and my mother takes some medicine that the even the pharmacy at the university hospital will no longer sell to Jews. Can you imagine? My father was the chief of the surgery department, succeeded by Jack. And now we are like beggars, scrounging for basic needs."

Although the Weinbergs in Lwów were not personally engulfed in life under Hitler, they were fully cognizant of his known hatred of Jews and the actions he had already taken toward achieving his dream of ridding his ever-expanding European turf of them. And they cringed at the nonchalance with which world leaders were letting him have his way. They closely followed news reports about the Munich conference that in effect gave Hitler carte blanche to devour Czechoslovakia. They felt sickened by the newspaper photo of Britain's Prime Minister

Neville Chamberlain arrival home waving the agreement he labeled a guarantee of "peace in our time." In November on Kristallnacht, the "Night of Broken Glass," the Nazis systematically destroyed and looted synagogues and Jewish homes and businesses in Germany and Austria. What more proof would anyone need of Hitler's intentions to wipe out the Jews?

A few weeks later Elisabeth called. Chanah answered the phone.

"How is Lily?"

"She is fine. Here, you can talk to her for just a quick second. The call is expensive," said Aunt Elisabeth.

"Hello, Chanah," said Lily. "We haven't seen each other in almost two years. I'm eight now."

"I know," Chanah said. "I wish we could play again. Maybe you will come to visit. It's okay. My Papa will send you the money."

"I don't think so. Mama just told me I'm going to London. Here's Mama. Goodbye, Chanah."

Elisabeth was back on the line.

"Please get your Papa or Mama, Chanah. Thank you."

Chanah gave the phone to her father.

"Lily is going to London," she said.

"What? Hello, Elisabeth. Chanah says Lily is going to London. Will you go, too? Your parents have finally become sensible and changed their minds?"

"No, unfortunately. But Lily has an opportunity for a place on the kindertransport. Have you heard of this?"

"I haven't," said Chaim.

"England has temporarily raised its quota on the number of Jews it will allow into the country to bring in 10,000 children. It was not easy to secure a place for her, but a friend in Warsaw with some influence got her a spot. She leaves tomorrow. At least one of us might be saved."

"Don't say that," said Chaim. "There is still hope. Maybe even Yankel—I mean Jack . . ."

"No. That's really the reason I called. About a month ago I heard he died in Dachau. A heart attack just like that. I don't believe it for a moment. At thirty-eight? Someone who took such good care of himself having a heart attack? I'm sure he was beaten or tortured or something else happened to damage his health. With his arrogance who knows how he behaved in the camp?"

"Oh, Elisabeth, I'm so sorry for you and Lily. Why didn't you call us right away after you heard the news? Not that it would change anything, of course, and you were under no obligation."

"Thank you for saying that, Chaim. I waited to call until I had done some checking to get more information about what happened. The first I heard of his death was from a friend whose husband was released but had heard the news about Jack from rumors in the camp after seeing him one morning for the last time. I didn't get official notification for a while. Then there was Kristallnacht—you heard about it, I suppose?"

"Yes. Horrible, outrageous."

"And after that all of my energy has been spent making the arrangements to get Lily out of here."

"Are you able to pay for her passage? We could help," said Chaim.

"You are so kind, kinder than I deserve after all the years I went along with Jack's nasty stubbornness about your parents and the rest of the family. Who would have thought that he, who would have preferred not to be Jewish, would die because he was? Well, that doesn't matter now. I thank you for your generous offer, but my friend in Warsaw is also helping to pay for Lily's trip."

"And she will go to your sister? Does she have a family?"

"Yes, she and her husband have two sons who are older than Lily, teen-agers, but she will have a good life with them. Chaim, perhaps I'm overstepping, but maybe you should consider sending Chanah and Shlomo to England?"

"I understand the intent of the suggestion, but at this point we wouldn't consider this. Besides, we have no family in England."

"My sister and her husband would, I'm sure, welcome them; if they couldn't take them into their home permanently, they would find caring friends to do it, I can assure you. Chaim, you and Esther understand what's happening, don't you? Do you think you're immune in Poland? You know where Hitler will go next."

"Elisabeth, we're more than aware. In Lwów, believe me, with the Poles and the Ukrainians, we hardly need Hitler. They're happy to pounce on the Jews anytime and they're salivating for his blessing to really unleash. But I just can't imagine doing what you suggest right now. And I'm sure Esther would never agree to it."

"I understand," she said, "and it breaks my heart to say goodbye to Lily. But I can't let her be a victim just because her grandparents are so blind to reality. I'm torn. They're old, they need me, they have no one else. My twin brother went to Shanghai. I don't blame him. You can only imagine how ridiculous my parents think that is. But that is pretty much the only place left, and just getting out of Austria to go there is harder than it was even a few months ago. My parents are barely speaking to me about my plan to send Lily, even though we're now living in the same apartment. I'm not even sure they or I could leave anymore, or if we could get into England. But Lily has to be saved."

The desperation in her voice disturbed Chaim so profoundly that his family, huddled nearby on the sofa, saw him wipe tears from his eyes. Shlomo and Chanah had never witnessed their father crying.

"Goodbye, Elisabeth. Good luck with everything. Please call whenever you want."

Chaim hung up the phone and turned to the inquiring faces in front of him.

"Yankel has died in the Dachau concentration camp. They told her it was a heart attack. Lily is going to London on some kind of special travel pass for Jewish children. Kindertransport it's called."

"Can she afford to send her? I thought she didn't have much money any more," said Esther.

"An influential friend in Warsaw got Lily a place and helped pay for it."

"Tanski," said Esther, "it must be Nachman Tanski. Somehow, even as a Jew, he has connections with business people and governments all over."

"Maybe," Chaim said. "But her parents still refuse to accept the danger of Hitler. They won't budge. Her brother has gone to Shanghai. Her sister lives in London, so that's where Lily will go. Poor Elisabeth is trapped between her duty to her parents and her longing to survive. But she's determined that Lily will. She even asked me . . . never mind."

"Tell me," said Esther.

Chaim glanced at the children to indicate this was a conversation he did not intend to have in their presence and inclined his head as if to indicate to Esther they needed to go into another room. When she got the hint and walked toward their bedroom, he followed and closed the door.

"She asked me to consider sending Shlomo and Chanah to London. She said her friend could probably get them passage, too. I told her no, but what do you think, Esther?"

"So far the situation here is not as grave as in Vienna," she said.

"Not yet, but you know we're in the Nazis' sights eventually. And it doesn't look like any one politician or any country has the chutzpah or the power to stop him from taking over all of Europe. We Jews are expendable."

"I know, I know. But we have to face this together. As a family," she said. "The children aren't going anywhere without us, and we're not going anywhere without them. What? Send Chanah away like the Golden Rosa?"

Esther's logic amused Chaim. The young martyr of the beautiful synagogue named for her for saving the building for her community, despite sacrificing her life in the process. A little far-fetched, but

Esther had made her point: Chanah and her brother were not going anywhere. They would stick together as a family. In solidarity he agreed with this decision while silently wondering if it really was for the best.

Chapter 10

Nine months, almost to the day, after Chaim's last conversation with his sister-in-law in Vienna, Hitler's forces invaded Poland. The Polish army defended Lwów against the Germans, but the disposition of conquered territory, presuming the easy and inevitable defeat of the Poles, had been predetermined by the Molotov-Ribbentrop Pact between Germany and the Soviet Union. Hitler took the West; Stalin's share, Eastern Poland, encompassed Lwów.

While the Weinbergs and their fellow Jews acknowledged their lot in life would be worse under the Nazis, it was immediately clear that the Soviets were not to be trusted. The terms of Lwów's surrender that included safe passage for captured Polish officers was instantly violated as the NKVD, the Soviet secret police, came to town and arrested them; many were sent to gulags deep into Russia, but most would be executed in 1940 at the infamous massacre in Katyn. The city became part of Soviet Ukraine and the capital of Lviv Oblast (province). And therefore named Lviv.

However, the fate of the Polish officers was of little concern, compared to day-to-day challenges. Jews and non-Jews alike were struck by the primitive boorishness of regular Soviet soldiers, as well as their skinny, unkempt looks and the shabbiness of their uniforms. Somehow, this did not match the vision of the shiny, advanced state depicted in the propaganda they had seen and read. But soon official socialist policy, as well as unofficial looting and confiscation, altered peoples' lives. Larger homes were converted into smaller, more densely inhabited ones. Food grew scarce. Communist contempt for religion restricted worship and closed religious schools.

The Weinberg brothers and their wives escaped the so-called nationalization of real estate, and each couple kept its own apartment. The Berkowski business operated by Esther and Chaim remained open, the shop overflowing with stock from her family's Warsaw store. Esther's parents and her brother's family had shipped what they could just ahead of the German invasion and their own planned escape. The goods had had better luck than the family, who did not leave in time and by fall 1940 found themselves residents of the Warsaw Ghetto. Esther spoke constantly of what would become of her aged parents and her brother, his wife, and three daughters. News was harder and harder to get.

Obviously, the local market for any of the Judaica, even the most prosaic mass-produced Kiddush cups or Shabbat challah bread plates, had become non-existent. As for the more valuable antique silver objects and rare books and manuscripts collected and used in wealthy homes or in synagogues, the shop might have been a museum. Even wealthy Jews were saving their money, and Gentile buyers rarely frequented the Berkowski shop, despite its upscale location within the Old City walls around the corner from the Rynok Square. Communication with overseas buyers was sporadic at best. Chaim and Esther tried valiantly to at least unload their cache of secular paintings by such Polish artists as Kozakiewicz; these were the only works any longer displayed in the front windows. Foot traffic had dribbled to a handful of citizens scurrying by with their heads down, minding their business, anxious to get to work or home. The Soviet presence did not promote leisurely strolling or window shopping. Which made the appearance of an apparently enlightened occupier from the East so startling to both Weinbergs tending the deserted store one day in early January of 1941.

Short and fair with an improbably czar-like goatee and turned out in a spotless uniform perfectly tailored to his muscular body, Colonel Semyon Zagoravich treated Chaim and Esther with utmost deference, even bowing his head a bit as a looked around. He showed only faint interest in any of the Kozakiewicz paintings in the window, though he said the fact that his sister in Kiev owned one had drawn him in. Inexplicably, old Hebrew books piled on a table caught his eye, and he began thumbing through one.

Trying to be equally nonchalant despite the minor terror that a Soviet officer was perusing her business, Esther inquired why he had picked up this particular volume. The officer explained that his best chum growing up was Jewish, and he, the colonel, used to like to compare the Hebrew alphabet to the Cyrillic.

"Of course, they aren't really similar at all, but I was fascinated by his study of Torah. I was supposed to attend his Bar Mitzvah, but his family left Russia before it happened. It was 1917. Remarkably, we remain in contact," the colonel said.

Surprised, Chaim asked where this friend was now.

"New York. He has recently opened a shop like yours. He says he already has clients who are very wealthy individuals. Even synagogues have begun to buy from him. Universities and scholars. Looking especially for items from Europe. You should contact him. I don't mean any disrespect, but perhaps with the state of things you should consider selling off your inventory."

"The 'state of things'," said Esther. "You mean our very slow business?"

"Yes, that and . . ." He inclined his head toward the street, where two men in suits and overcoats were dragging another man between them.

"You mean, we're on some list to be arrested? You know something about us?" Chaim's face turned red as he pleaded for answer.

"No, don't worry, I know nothing. I am a man of medicine, a

surgeon. It's just that these are unpredictable times. One never knows what the next day will bring."

"That is for sure," said Esther. "If you would be so kind as to contact your friend, we would be most appreciative."

When Zagoravich left, she turned to her husband and said, "It certainly can't hurt to have a friend in the Soviet army."

"For now. Who knows how long he will be on the winning side?"

Chanah sat in back of the counter doing her schoolwork.

"What do you mean by that, Papa? The Nazis?"

Esther and Chaim looked at each other. They had long since figured there was no point in pretending there was a bright and secure future ahead for the family.

The status quo of Soviet rule, tense and uncertain as it was, collapsed on June 22, 1941, when Hitler's forces launched Operation Barbarossa, the tyrant's drive to surpass Europe's last ambitious conqueror, Napoleon Bonaparte, in vanquishing Russia. Colonel Zagoravich had warned Chaim the week before that his "sources" reported the Germans were gearing up for an eastern drive, despite the agreement with the USSR in 1939.

By this time the Berkowski shop was closed. Thanks to Zagoravich's friend, most of the inventory had been shipped to New York. Chaim and Esther had accumulated a cash reserve that might have paid for transit out of harm's way, if there was somewhere to go. Even Shanghai was no longer an option. The logistics alone were impossible, as feasible train and shipping routes were mostly memories now. Some of their friends had left the city for the East in the unofficial company of the retreating Soviet Army. Chaim begged Esther to consider this, but she had recently undergone surgery for the removal of her gallbladder and did not feel strong enough to pack up their belongings and organize the journey. Nonsense, her husband, said, we don't need much. And wouldn't be able to take much, anyway. One suitcase each. He felt sure the colonel would help them but hesitated to contact him without Esther's full endorsement of leaving. It would be insincere to make arrangements and then not follow through. He could not do that to his friend, who would likely be risking a lot to help the Weinbergs.

On June 29 there was a knock on the door of their apartment. Chaim opened it a crack, and was surprised to find Zagoravich standing there in a summer business suit, holding a felt hat in his hands. He assumed the officer had already departed with his military comrades fleeing the advancing Germans.

"Come in, come in, Semyon, and sit down. Esther, get the colonel a glass of cold tea. What can we do for you? And why are you still in Lviv? Hitler broke the agreement with Stalin. That was probably to be predicted, but now the Germans will be here any day."

"Comrade Stalin never completely trusted Hitler, I'm sure," said Zagoravich. "He's too smart for that. And certainly Hitler didn't trust Stalin. Or care. Two tough guys playing at the same game."

"I am relieved to see you, my friend, still alive and well. But, again, why are you still here?"

"I have just finished my duties caring for the wounded we are loading up to leave. There is space for you and your family in vehicles under my control. All four of you. But you must come with me now. The convoy will depart in three hours."

Chaim looked at his wife and saw her gazing around the room as if to take inventory of everything in it—the furniture, glass and porcelain collectibles, their own remaining silver ritual objects resplendent on shelves of an Art Deco china cabinet, and paintings on the walls, including the Kozakiewicz. What a brouhaha it had started at that last family celebration less than five years ago, but a lifetime in terms of the people and the existence that had slipped away since then. Chaim cherished Esther's many fine qualities as a wife, mother, and businesswoman but knew how much she also loved her fine possessions. Not as much as him or her children, he told himself, but there was that materialistic tendency that would be a problem.

She spoke first, "But, Semyon, I'm barely recovered from my surgery. I don't think I can travel."

"I'm a surgeon myself, as you know, Esther," he said, "I would personally supervise you on the trip and make sure to make you as comfortable as possible."

"But to take only one suitcase. None of this . . ." She gestured around the room.

"Esther," said Chaim. "We would take what's important. The children and ourselves. Furniture and clothes we can always get."

Chanah and Shlomo were astounded by the conversation. A journey east into Russia sounded like a huge adventure to them, and they knew the arrival of the Nazis would bring even more hardship than had been afflicted on them by the Russians. By this time they were thirteen and seventeen, respectively, hardly children.

"Maybe you should go and take Shlomo," Esther said. "Chanah will stay here with me."

"We could use Shlomo to fight with us," said Zagoravich.

"That's one thing I'm afraid of," Chaim said.

"Consider the fate of a strong, handsome, young Jewish man when the Germans arrive," the Russian said.

The colonel had made his point. Still, Chaim could not believe he was even considering leaving his wife and daughter behind. And that Esther had suggested it.

"Esther, are you sure? I would send for you and Chanah as soon as we reach safety."

The colonel nodded, though that could be a hollow promise. Safety? Who knew where or when there would be safety? With Hitler's forces in hot pursuit? The Germans were obviously not planning to stop until they had triumphed over the vast expanse of the Soviet Union all the way to Moscow and Leningrad. Zagoravich would never express the opinion publicly or even in the privacy of his closest family or comrades, but he had no confidence Stalin's military would be successful in pushing the Germans back and dealing Hitler's soldiers the same fate as Napoleon's.

"Yes, Chaim. You and Shlomo, go and pack your suitcases. I will prepare some food for you to take with you."

Two hours later the colonel returned. They all descended to the street, where a driver waited next to an ambulance. Chaim and Shlomo kissed and embraced Esther and Chanah and climbed into the back of the vehicle; a sleeping soldier with bandaged head and a nurse were already ensconced in there for the trip. Zagoravich climbed into the front seat next to the driver.

As the ambulance moved away down Słoneczna Street and turned the corner, Chanah looked at her sobbing mother and wondered why this was happening.

"I thought the important thing was to stick together as a family," she said.

"Circumstances," her mother said. "We have to be flexible."

"Just like you were about packing up and leaving in a hurry."

"But I'm barely out of the hospital, Chanah. The ride would have killed me."

"It's been three weeks, Mama. The colonel is a doctor. There was a nurse in the ambulance. You just couldn't manage to leave with only one suitcase."

Esther was shocked that her daughter would speak to her like that, even if a twinge of guilt was coming over her.

"Chanah, why are you tormenting me so? Your father took it upon himself to leave. Why don't you blame him?"

Chanah shrugged. She loved her mother but was adult enough to recognize her flaws and to realize she, the child, would likely become the protector and caregiver of the mother. It was too soon for her to acknowledge her anger with her father for taking her brother and not her. She was stuck in Lwów, probably trapped. She remembered how strong Bubbe was in the face of losing Uncle Yankel and Zayde. She thought about the test faced by the Golden Rosa, confronting the Jesuits on behalf of her people. The Nazis were going to be Chanah's test. She did not need to be a heroine, just keep her mother and herself alive.

The Nazis took Lwów on June 29, 1941. Even before they could fully gear up their anti-Jewish administrative tactics, the Ukrainians took it upon themselves to welcome the conquerors with an old-fashioned pogrom, a local tradition repeated often in the city's history. The excuse, as if they needed one, was the totally illogical allegation that Jews participated in the execution of four thousand political prisoners, a massacre perpetrated by the Soviets on their way out of town.

The murderous riots unfolded under the watch and with the blessing of anyone sporting any sort of uniform of authority. Random Jews on the street were beaten and brutalized, pushed to their knees to scrub the pavement, many nearly or totally naked, having been forcibly stripped of their clothing as the first humiliation. Chanah, a young-looking thirteen, had just come out of a "friendly" food market when she witnessed one of her Jewish schoolmates, physically more mature for her age, running down the street pursued by a mob grabbing at her dress until the sympathetic elderly Gentile grocer seized her and pulled her into the safety of his store, locking its door and lowering metal shutters. The ruffians leading the mob turned and fixed their gaze on Chanah, momentarily frozen into a standstill. Mercifully, they ran off in pursuit of other prey.

She heard one say, "Nah, we can't touch one of ours."

The blonde hair. Though grateful to be safe, she could not shake a sense of shame about escaping for the simple reason she didn't fit some stupid Ukrainian's concept of a Jewish stereotype. She ran home and told her mother the story of what she saw on the street. Esther thought it was the trauma of that incident and fear for her own well-being that sustained her daughter's tears. She did not understand Chanah's internal conflict.

"Be glad for your blonde hair, my darling," she said. "But now shush. Papa just sent a letter from Russia. He and Shlomo arrived in

Odessa. The sea is so beautiful at this time of year. Zagoravich found him and Shlomo a room with a cousin of his and moved on further east. There are many Poles who have settled in Odessa. The Nazis are not there yet."

"They will be," said Chanah.

"Why must you be so pessimistic, Chanah?"

"Realistic, Mama. Realistic."

"You're strong. Maybe like you said Bubbe was. You told us, and you were right. Though, thank God, she and Zayde didn't live long enough to see what's happening now."

Bubbe would have faced it better than you, thought Chanah. She would have picked up her suitcase and left with Papa and Shlomo.

Chapter 11

Chanah's Uncle Nathan was one of two partners in a company that manufactured men's clothing. The other owner of the business was a Polish-Catholic man named Anton Nowakowski, who had grown up in the same apartment building as the Weinberg brothers. Anton and Nathan had served together in the Polish Army. After the Great War they scraped up the money to buy this business from the widow of its founder. The arrangement had worked out well. Anton oversaw the operations inside the factory, and the affable Nathan was the outside salesman.

Freya Weinberg, though childless herself, was a teacher and principal at a Jewish high school that taught Hebrew and Yiddish language and literature and promoted the Zionist ideal of developing Palestine into a Jewish homeland. When the Soviets came, the official curriculum they imposed at all schools eliminated Hebrew and Yiddish in the Jewish schools and substituted formal classes in the Ukrainian language. Yet, other than in the schools, this was a brief window in which Yiddish cultural life continued to thrive in the city, largely due to the arrival of more than 100,000 refugees from western, Nazi-occupied, Poland, who swelled the Jewish population of newly renamed Lviv to 220,000. Once the Nazis came, however, it was all moot: the Jewish schools would never reopen after the summer break, and surely no one was even thinking about going to the theatre.

Chanah was a student at Aunt Freya's school and respected her aunt very much. Freya, obviously, was much more intellectual than Esther, and she equally enjoyed spending time with her niece, whose mind was very sharp and who absorbed facts and ideas quickly. Chanah was a star student but was sometimes accused of getting special treatment because her aunt was the principal. Her aunt tried very hard to negate that impression in school; their special times together were out of school on evenings and weekends. Theatre, concerts, bookstores, museums—these were outings in which Chanah's mother was less interested than Freya. Conversation with Aunt Freya was more stimulating the older Chanah got. Esther may have been jealous but she concealed it, knowing Chanah's interests tended to match Freya's more than her own and grateful Chanah had a soul mate in these times when friendships, between adults or children, were fraying under the external pressures besetting most people they knew. Social circles in Lwów, or Lviv under the Soviets, had always been insular. Now, in the place that had been rechristened the Austro-Germanic Lemberg, families facing the Nazi onslaught were too preoccupied with life and death to even pretend that maintaining the niceties of outside relationships mattered anymore. Trust quickly broke down in the Jewish community when certain of its members were hand-picked to "volunteer" as leaders of the Judenrat council to help administer and enforce the Nazis' edicts.

It had taken little more than a week before all Jews over the age of fourteen were ordered to wear white armbands displaying blue Stars of David. Freya and Nathan dodged this early distinction because of their association with Anton, Nathan's partner, who quickly acceded to a lucrative German requisition of the factory for the manufacture of Wehrmacht uniforms. The transformation of the business included Anton's acquisition, at a bargain price, of Nathan's half of the partnership. Nathan could stay on as an employee in the office.

The end of July brought yet another riotous pogrom in a month of such uprisings that became known as the Petliura Days, commemorating the legacy of the anti-Semitic Ukrainian politician Symon Petliura assassinated in the 1920s by a Jewish anarchist. Relative quiet on the streets was a deceptive lull for Jews, who only left their homes in search of increasingly diminishing food and whatever other basic supplies they might find.

With her fair appearance Chanah was her mother's primary messenger to the outer world. There had been no word from Chaim and Shlomo in months. Having worked alongside her husband in the business her family established, Esther was unaccustomed to staying home cooped up, especially in a household so contracted. She spent hours arranging and rearranging the knickknacks on her shelves, the clothes in her closet, and the pots and pans and meager foodstuffs in the pantry. Chanah, when she wasn't at Aunt Freya's house, escaped reality and her mother's noisy puttering through the books her aunt brought home from the school; with nothing else to do, she managed to finish *War and Peace* that summer. Even a thirteen-year-old reader recognized that this was an ironically timely choice as the Germans swept toward Russia like Napoleon.

Early in November the word went out that Jews had to move into a ghetto within the next month. Esther began to catalogue her belongings to figure out what was worth taking and hired a delivery service for the move. Chanah, in disbelief, spent more and more time at Aunt Freya's—Nathan and Freya were exempt from this mandate, too—so she was there one day when the Nazis decided to speed up the moving process and forcibly hustle Jews toward their new neighborhood. This was reported to her aunt in a phone call from a friend who lived down the block from Chanah and her mother and had seen Esther being herded onto an open half-track vehicle directing the delivery man to follow her.

"I need to go," said Chanah.

"No, you stay here."

"But what will Mama do without me?"

When Uncle Nathan came home at three o'clock, his wife knew there was more news. He sat his niece down to tell her Esther had argued with a German officer about her assigned placement in a two-room ghetto apartment she and Chanah would share with three generations, ranging in age from three months to seventy-six, of a family of six. She had created quite a scene. How would her things fit there? As she ran out of the tenement back to the street, where her driver waited with his horse-drawn wagon piled high with furniture and suitcases, the officer in charge caught her in his grasp and threw her to the ground. Struggling to her feet, Esther did not see him take out his gun. She fell back onto the pavement. The officer signaled to the driver to get out of there. When he protested he had not been paid for his service, the officer shot him, too.

"He should have known not to work for a cheap Jew. Come down and get her out of here," the Nazi said, motioning to the few Jews brave enough to watch from their windows.

Nathan had heard Esther's body was wedged onto a cart already stacked with corpses. No one knew where it went after the makeshift hearse moved away from the site. The nearby Poltva River tunnel was the best guess. As for her belongings, as soon as the German officer and his posse moved on, the newly arrived denizens of the ghetto descended upon it and fought for its contents. None of them had had the foresight or the gall to prepare as well as Esther; seeing it did not turn out well for her, they thanked God they hadn't, but there was no reason not to help themselves to her possessions after the fact.

"Mama, Mama. I must go to find her . . . her body," Chanah screamed as her aunt and uncle held her tightly in a futile effort to calm her.

"No," said Nathan. "You must stay here. We don't have to move to the ghetto."

"Yet," Aunt Freya said.

Chanah's uncle said, "Tomorrow Anton and his wife will go over and see if there are any of your things left to get out of there. If the Germans left anything you can use."

"I can go. I know where everything is," said Chanah.

Aunt Freya was adamant.

"No, it's too dangerous. You're safe here. You're not going back to your house, you're not going anywhere for now. The Nazis certainly knew that you lived with your mother, but you weren't there when they came to get her. They might be looking out for you."

Chanah had no choice but to accept this.

The next evening Anton and his wife Stefania pulled up and brought in two suitcases of clothes and books they had managed to collect for Chanah from the remnants left behind after the apartment was pillaged.

"It was a mess. Lots of broken glass. That cabinet Esther and Chaim had with all the silver and china. Emptied and pulled down. But there is one thing they didn't take. I need your help, Nathan, to carry it in."

The A. Kozakiewicz painting. The gold frame was cracked, as if someone had tried to wrest it off and given up.

Aunt Freya laughed, which broke the silent tension, as everyone stared at her unable to figure out what could be remotely humorous at that moment.

"Maybe Yankel was right. Even the Nazis didn't want this picture . . ."

Chapter 12

By the end of 1942 it was clear to Freya and Nathan they could not count indefinitely on the protection afforded to them by Anton and the uniform factory. Nathan saw the eyes of the Nazi-appointed foreman, a Ukrainian named Andruko, fixed on his every move and figuratively drawing a bull's eye on his back. Whenever a higher-up German visited the plant, Nathan's queasiness competed with his natural inclination to avoid eye contact with the enemy. To increase production to a breakneck pace the Germans insisted that the factory adopt an operational schedule of twenty-four hours a day, seven days a week. There were not enough employees to give everyone any semblance of a normal schedule of shifts. Even the addition to the work force of sixteen Jewish men and six Jewish women ferried across the city every day from their new homes in the ghetto or at Janowska, a work camp established on the outskirts of town, did not alleviate the long, grueling hours. These were employees only there as cogs along the assembly line; prisoners were not added to the payroll.

Nathan was acquainted with a few of them, or their families, and he knew his presence in the office, despite his diminished status at the company, gave the newcomers the impression he was a collaborationist as surely as if he were the hand-picked leader of the *Judenrat* selecting Jews for the deportations that had begun the previous March. Belzec, a village less than ninety kilometers away, was the rumored destination. Anton, his former partner and now his boss, outwardly conformed to the wishes of the real bosses but privately did as much as he could to ease the daily difficulties of life for Freya, Nathan, and Chanah, who were unique among Jews still living in their own apartment in the city. He transported Nathan to and from work every day, and, assisted by Stefania, made sure the Weinbergs had enough food and rudimentary household supplies. These were in short supply for even non-Jewish civilians, but as owners of a business contributing to the German war effort, the Nowakowskis had enough to share.

Freya, at home with Chanah, kept the two of them busy reading and discussing books, mending the clothes that were increasingly threadbare, and devising meals out of the limited ingredients surreptitiously provided them. There was simply not much else to do. The advent of the warmer weather, formerly a blissful time after the frigid winters, brought no relief this year. Despite the protection of the factory affiliation, for Freya alone to escape the building for a breath of air—never mind a walk to the park—seemed too much of a risk. Chanah felt less threatened but rarely ventured out on her own to save her aunt from worry. Occasionally, though, the monotony and staleness of the indoors compelled her to slip out.

One day at the end of May, while her aunt lay down for a nap, she not only left the building but boarded the trolley to the center of the city. Lemberg retained the familiar bloom of springtime renewal, and the now fourteen-year-old Chanah cherished every sight and feel of the flowers on the Rynok she had taken for granted her whole life. Fourteen meant she should have been wearing the white Star of David armband, as did her Uncle Nathan at the factory, but she had never acquired one and she saw no one on the street wearing one as she walked along. Of course, signs and symbols of change abounded, as swastikas adorned banners, posters, and the uniforms of the ubiquitous Germans and the insignia of their local henchmen, the *Ukrainische Hilfspolizei*, armed and carrying batons, only too willing to serve.

Two jowly, beer-bellied members of this squad, stationed outside an ice cream shop and eating chocolate cones, benignly gave her a leering once-over as she entered, but a blonde, crew-cutted younger recruit bowed slightly to make a ceremony of deferring to her as she approached the counter to order from the young woman server trying to vie for his attention. Chanah paid and ate her fresh strawberry sundae on a park bench in solitary and unmolested reverie. The trauma of losing her mother; of not knowing what had happened to her father and brother; and of being cooped up with a caring aunt and uncle who would not even attempt to spend the afternoon like this slipped away for a few minutes. A loud whining siren broke the trance, and the car emitting it stopped in front of the ice cream parlor to pick up a boy of about ten, wearing shorts and a newsboy cap, being dragged from the adjacent alley by the courtly young auxiliary policeman. A small crowd of onlookers was cheering, and Chanah distinctly heard "get Jew baby" before surreptitiously rising from the bench and running for the approaching trolley to go home. It was of small comfort that the ride back was uneventful as she raced up to the apartment.

"Thank goodness, you're back," said Aunt Freya. "What could you possibly have been thinking, Chanah, going out by yourself? Where have you been?"

"I went downtown, took a walk, ate an ice cream sundae. Just like a normal person, like I used to do," said Chanah.

"But these are not normal times," Freya said. "I was frantic when I woke up."

"I'm sorry to have frightened you, I truly am. But I had no problems. No one bothered me. A young policeman even bowed to me and let me go ahead of him in line at the ice cream shop. It was funny. The girl behind the counter was jealous, I could tell."

"So, you're telling me, Chanahh, you can pass? Does that make you happy? Do you think it's a good idea to test your luck? You must promise me not to do it again. I would never forgive myself if something happened to you, if you were snatched off the street by the Nazis."

"I promise, Auntie, I won't."

I guess I really do look like a *shikseh,* Chanah thought. It got me a trolley ride and an ice cream, but what kind of Jewish girl would do that? It doesn't make me a heroine like Queen Esther or the Golden Rosa.

The following week Uncle Nathan brought home a letter mailed to his office from his wife's sister Rachael, who had left Lwów ten years before and moved to Jerusalem. Receiving mail at home was too dangerous, so this rare piece of communication from the outside world was a treasure. Freya closed her eyes as she grasped the envelope and held it in both hands for a second before even ripping it open.

"I thought I'd wait until I got home to let you read it first," Nathan said. "Besides, I don't want to give Andruko any excuse to ask questions. What's that? Who's it from? He'd be all over me and the letter. Anton slipped the envelope to me in the washroom."

"She says there's a rumor that Hitler wants to get the German Templars out of Palestine. Maybe even exchange them for some Jews in Europe. Some of the Templars are Nazis, and the British are rounding them up and deporting them to places like Australia. Rachael wants to know if we still have our Palestine passports. That would help us be included in the exchange."

Freya and Nathan had traveled to Palestine in 1936 to visit Rachael and her husband, Avraham, and an aunt and uncle and cousins who had moved there, some settling in Jerusalem and a few heartier pioneers working in the fields of the burgeoning kibbutz movement. With the Nazis already in power in Germany and the outlook bleak for realistic European Jews, the family there urged the visitors to obtain passports from the ruling British Mandate in the Holy Land.

"Just in case," said Rachael, "a safety precaution. Although I don't know why you would want to go back to Lwów, anyway. You have no children. Stay!"

Freya tried to persuade her husband to make the move. They both enjoyed the trip and stayed from November until Purim, traveling throughout the small country. The weather alone was a break from their home in Poland, and it was such a treat to bathe in the Mediterranean in winter. But practical and family matters worried

Nathan. How would they earn a living? His parents were elderly and depended on both him and his brother Chaim for support. Europe was bad, but there were political problems in Palestine, too. The Arabs were violently rioting, the British were not exactly lovers of the Jews. The future would be uncertain. Would they be any better off?

Freya could not totally disagree and she bowed to her husband's reasoning. But the positive spirit of most people they met and the intangible uplift she felt in Jerusalem motivated her to persuade Nathan to get the passports.

"Just in case."

Although Chanah had never heard about any dilemma her aunt and uncle had regarding a move to Palestine—or about the passports—she remembered they had brought her a little silver filigree bracelet that no longer fit her now adult-sized wrist, as well as a book of photographs of the walled Old City of Jerusalem, the new Hebrew University perched on a hill there, the desert, the seaside, people holding up oranges amid the trees growing them. The book's paper cover had been ripped when the Nazis visited her home the day they took her mother, but it was left on the floor and returned to her in a box when Anton and Stefania retrieved the remaining belongings in her old room. She was surprised to see it but figured it wasn't precious enough for the Nazis to bother with. And they were too stupid to care about books.

The passports were hidden in Aunt Freya's lingerie drawer. After reading the letter from her sister, she went into her bedroom and fished them out.

"Here they are," she said. "Now what? How do we get into this exchange? Do you think the officers who supervise the factory could help?"

"Not Andruko, of course, but maybe one of the Germans who comes every Monday morning. Schwarzkopf. Not too bad a fellow, compared to most of them," said Nathan. "This may be the time to consider Palestine, if we could actually get there."

"'Consider Palestine'? I'd consider anywhere to get out of here. The planet Mars. The Moon," Freya said. "We should have gone when we could get out legally, with new passports in hand."

"You're right, Freya," her husband said. "We should have. We should have done a lot of things we didn't do. I'm sorry. I promise I will look into this. No doubt, we need to take advantage of any possible opportunity to get out. But, Freya, please, your bitterness doesn't help. We've come this far and survived. Let's try to do the best we can. But with love and support for each other. For ourselves and for Chanah."

Chanah had never known her aunt and uncle to squabble like this but was relieved to be mentioned at the end of the argument and apparently part of the equation in this plan for an escape from the Nazis. But she was curious about the idea of an exchange with a people she had never heard of.

"Who are the German Templars?"

Freya explained they were a community of messianic German Christians who had lived in the Holy Land since the last century. They worked the land and established residential German colonies in the cities, too, large ones in Haifa and Jerusalem. Now they were embued with Nazism, especially some of the younger Templars who had been sent to study in Germany. As enemies of the British who ruled Palestine, many had been interned in prisoner-of-war camps.

Chanah did not understand one key word her aunt had used.

"What does messianic mean?"

"For them it means," said Nathan, "the second coming of Jesus Christ. He is their Messiah. His return is the dream that inspires the Templars to cultivate the land and build Palestine. To prepare for his return."

"Like the Jews work the land to prepare for a Jewish homeland? There won't be both."

"You're right, Chanah," said her aunt. "The Jews who dream the Zionist dream. Like us. Now, if this exchange plan works, we can be part of making this dream come true. One hopes it's more realistic than the reappearance of Christ or of a Jewish Messiah."

A few days later, however, the dream of escaping as part of the exchange for the German Templars blurred back into the current nightmare. Nathan learned through German channels connected to the overseers of the factory that Jewish candidates for the exchange with the Templars would first be funneled through a concentration camp in Germany, Bergen Belsen—"for processing"—a stop along the way that portended risk. In their ecstasy of relief and gratitude to have found an escape route, Nathan and Freya had allowed themselves not to consider there might be any pitfalls, an error of naiveté when one was dealing with the Germans. Worse, absolutely no one without a Palestine passport in hand would be eligible even to join the transport to Bergen Belsen, which somehow sounded more attractive than the destinations of the current transports of Jews out of Lwów.

When he returned home from the factory after getting this clarification, Nathan said nothing about the details, though conversation about leaving for Palestine had been the only thing they really ever talked about any more. The three of them ate their meager supper of meatless borscht Freya had concocted from the few overripe vegetables and potatoes and two-day-old bread Anton and Stefania had provided that week.

"Soon," said Freya, "we shall have all the vegetables we want and chickens and eggs straight from the farms . . ."

"And fresh oranges," said Chanah, "we can pick off the trees in the orchards in Palestine."

Nathan smiled but did not join the fantasizing. As much as he hated to spoil the joy of anticipation his wife and niece exuded, he knew he had no choice but to break the news that evening. The deadline to sign up for the exchange was only four days away. The Palestine passport requirement disqualified Chanah. He and Freya had to face the dilemma of staying or of leaving without her.

He had already discussed this with Anton at work. His former partner would, he said, gladly take Chanah to live in his home with his family, but the Germans who controlled the factory visited often, and the presence of a new addition to the household would raise suspicion, even if they introduced her as the maid. Nathan visibly winced at that comment. Anton, realizing how insensitive that sounded, slapped his forehead in contrition and offered another idea.

"The sister of Stefania's best friend is a nurse at the Catholic hospital. In the past she worked at the hospital on Rappaport Street."

"The Jewish hospital? I didn't know a Gentile would work there."

"She was assistant to the head doctor in the eye department. I've met her at their family gatherings. Seems to be a nice woman. From Krakow originally. Her husband was Ukrainian but died when her son was very young. The son has been in seminary studying to be a priest, even though Stefania says Jadwiga—that is her name—stopped going to church when the Soviets were here and hasn't gone back. Stefania says Jadwiga took bandages and medicine to the Jewish hospital when it was low on supplies before it closed. She herself has little money. The Germans have hospital workers on starvation wages, too. Maybe a place for your niece? Chanah doesn't look Jewish. She might survive in a good Polish home."

"Freya—no, I—could never do it. Leave Chanah here? My brother's daughter? She has already survived so much. Her parents and brother gone. No, Anton, thank you. We will stay here and take our chances."

"Nathan, don't be a fool. You and Freya have a chance to escape before the war is over. If you go to Palestine and make a home there, Chanah will have a place to go. She can be safe here in a good home, and you can come back for her and all live happily ever after."

"You make it sound so easy, Anton. I hope you're never faced with such a predicament."

"My friend," Anton patted Nathan on the shoulder, "believe me I understand. With the Nazis, even as they let me be the so-called boss of the place, who knows what will happen when they decide I'm no longer useful to them? Your future, if you stay here, is more certain—a trajectory toward doom. I'm not sure how long I can protect you. Every day I hear Andruko making some snide comment that 'the *Yid* Weinberg' is cheating in the accounts or spitting in the coffee pot or something equally ridiculous. Of course, I know there is no truth to this—we have been friends and partners for a long time—but he talks on the phone to I-don't-know-who . . ."

"Say no more. You have been a hero keeping me here and providing for my family. This problem is mine to solve."

That evening, mentally wrestling with the devil's bargains from which he had to choose, it was not difficult to feign a headache and go to bed early. Freya followed him into the bedroom, which was both predictable and exactly what he wanted and needed to happen.

"A headache. Here, a tablet and some water. Take it," she said.

"I don't really have a headache. Not the kind a tablet would help, anyway. Sit down, Freya, we have to decide what to do. Chanah can't go with us for the exchange."

"What do you mean she can't go with us? She's like our daughter, and we are all she has now."

"To even get on the train with us she has to have her own Palestine passport. And, by the way, the train will go to a concentration camp— Bergen Belsen inside Germany—before we can leave for Palestine to be exchanged. For processing, I'm told."

"What the Germans shine at—processing. We can't go, Nathan. That's it. I won't leave her."

"That's what I told Anton. He thinks we're foolish to stay, that we will be deported to one of the places from which no one is heard from again. He thinks we should leave Chanah here, get to Palestine, make a home for her, that with her looks she can survive here. He even knows a Christian woman he thinks would take her in and treat her well."

"What woman? Leave her here with some stranger? A Ukrainian?"

"No, a Polish woman, actually. From Krakow. A nurse, the sister of Stefania's best friend. She used to work at the Jewish hospital for the chief eye doctor. Before it closed, she sneaked supplies out of the Catholic hospital back there to help them. She sounds like a good person, Freya. Maybe we should consider it. Meet her. Anton and Stefania could bring her over. Tomorrow evening."

Freya moved off the bed and grabbed the Palestine passports that had been propped up against the mirror of her dressing table.

"Can't we find someone to make something that looks just like these?"

"A forger? Where would we find one? It's not like I can ask anyone at the factory or get out for lunch to check around. We are among the very few Jews still in the city. Certainly the only ones still in our own apartment with someone holding a job and getting paid. Our situation is phenomenally exceptional but it is hardly without restriction or risk. Any day the Nazis could decide I should be dispensed with, and Anton would not be able to stop them, as much as I do believe he would want to. The Jewish workers we had have been weeded out. There are only a few now, shuttled back and forth to the work camp at Janowska. The rest have been deported, to the best of our knowledge. All of them have been bled dry from the labor, practically no food . . . Even Anton, himself, not a Jew, is concerned about his own future, and his family's."

Other than Anton and Stefania bearing food and household supplies, the Weinbergs had not entertained any guests or even summoned a repairman since Chanah moved in. So, the next evening when the Nowakowskis escorted Jadwiga through the door, the apartment felt curiously full, almost festive for the very brief moment when she held out her own basket to a very guarded hostess. Freya lifted the cloth that covered its contents and withdrew a treat: a chocolate cake that smelled and felt tantalizingly warm from recent baking despite its concave shape, a testament to the universal rationing of flour. Underneath were the banal cabbage and potatoes that had constituted the household's monotonous daily menus for months, plus three eggs and a two-inch cube of hard cheese.

The generosity of this stranger was received with muttered thanks by Nathan and Freya. The woman, perhaps fifty-years-old, wore a wrinkled white nurse's uniform under a worn brown coat that concealed a bulky body; her shape reminded Chanah of the loving cuddliness of her late Bubbe. However, the visitor's thinning and obviously dyed red hair quickly shattered that association.

The woman made herself at home, plunking down on Nathan's favorite upholstered chair and taking appreciative note of her surroundings. The painting on the wall caught her eye.

"That picture," she said. "I like that artist very much. Kozakiewicz. I saw many of his in Poland."

"Well, he was Polish," said Chanah.

"Of course. You're a very smart young lady, just as your friends told me. You like books, you know about painters. Very good."

Chanah had absolutely no inkling who this woman was or why she was there. Just a friend of Anton and Stefania, she figured. But very odd to have a stranger here. Odder still, this Gentile stranger, who seemed so unaccountably and patronizingly interested in Chanah herself.

Freya and Nathan sat on the sofa with Chanah wedged between them and joined their arms together hugging her. Neither had been able to summon the gumption to tell her what might happen and they hoped their niece had not been alarmed by the cessation in the dinnertime conversation about Palestine. If she noticed, which they could not imagine she had not, she was savvy enough to know it may not have been something to count on or it was simply too wonderful to continue to discuss to tempt the evil eye and jinx the plan.

Of course, Chanah had sensed the change. In the two or three days before this gathering her aunt and uncle had not only stopped bringing up Palestine, squelching her inclination to broach the subject, but were generally quieter than usual and more visibly distressed, if that was possible, than at any time since German occupation began. Suddenly, Uncle Nathan had mysterious headaches. Aunt Freya, who normally kept herself busy even during her forced confinement in the apartment, spent countless hours staring into space and sighing. Sitting in their double embrace on the sofa was weird enough to prove to Chanah something had changed. She wished this gushy woman would leave so she ask them what was going on. Or tell them what she thought was happening.

She came right out with it the moment the door closed behind Jadwiga and the Nowakowskis.

"You're leaving me with that woman, aren't you?"

Freya and Nathan looked at each other and pointed her back to the sofa. They explained the Palestine passport situation and that the trip would start with a stay at a concentration camp before they would be exchanged for German Templars. They hated that Chanah would not be able to accompany them but promised to come back for her as soon as they reached Palestine and could return to Europe. With Jadwiga she would be safer than anywhere else. Chanah would be introduced as the daughter of a cousin who had died, she would be well treated, they would leave plenty of money for Jadwiga to take care of her, enough for a Christian woman to be able to buy better food and clothes for her. Things they could no longer do.

Both sobbed as they made their case. Chanah looked at them dry-eyed and snickered. If it was going to be so great, why were they crying? Obviously, this was a plan that upset them as much as it did her, despite her efforts to appear stoic. Everyone else had left her—her mother, her father, her brother—so she would just have to manage one more wrench away from her family. She knew why she was easy to leave: she was blonde and could pass.

Chanah would be strong. Bubbe would be proud. So would the Golden Rosa. If Uncle Nathan and Aunt Freya promised to come back for her, it would happen. She had to believe that.

A week later Anton and Stefania came to collect Chanah, two suitcases, a box of books, and the A. Kozakiewicz painting and drove her to a street in an area of the city she had never been. There Jadwiga greeted her, supervised Anton's unloading of the car, and held out her hand to receive the envelope full of cash the Weinbergs had given him before closing the door of Chanah's new home.

Two hours after they bade farewell to their niece, a Nazi officer picked up Freya and Nathan to convey them to the train for Bergen Belsen.

When Chanah unpacked in the small bedroom that Jadwiga said had been that of her son, the seminary student Pawel, she found a gold chain with a tiny Star of David Freya had slipped into her suitcase. There was also a pearl necklace that she remembered her mother Esther wearing. She folded them both into a pair of socks tucked in the bottom drawer of her new bureau.

By evening she had become Magdalena Wolska, a Catholic girl from the farm country near Krakow. The real Magdalena had been born and died the year before Chanah's birth, so the birth certificate was real enough to legitimize the residency papers she would carry. Jadwiga gave her a silver chain with a cross hanging on it and a catechism book and said she should call her Auntie.

PART III

Lviv, Ukraine
1995

Chapter 13

Our first morning in Lviv dawned grey and ugly. The windows in our hotel room were fogged with condensation that, combined with the lack of wattage in lamps and overhead lighting, only made the room darker and more claustrophobic. I had heard Simon on the phone with the travel planning minions at Mossad headquarters. They had done their best to match his request for an indoor pool for me, but the only option was too far from the center of the city and not a place we would want to stay, he said. Was he just being a travel snob?

"How bad could it be?"

"If we were Soviet *apparatchiks* traveling on government business, we'd think it was five-star," said Simon. "Sorry about the pool—or lack of same. At least this is reasonably comfortable and has some of that old-fashioned historic charm you usually love. It must be the best in town; you know the Mossad doesn't stint on creature comforts."

"I'll live," I said. "Just traipsing around in this cold will burn calories. Besides, I hope we won't be here too long. You know how fond I am about these Jewish graveyard cities, where there used to be thriving communities but now there are no Jews. Or very few."

"I know. Well, at least we have a mission and a head start on looking for The Duck and the codex and painting. Through his colleagues here Avi got the name of a friendly priest at the cathedral . . ."

"The Mossad has operatives here?"

Simon gave me that look and the hand gesture that jauntily said why ask such a foolish question.

"... and Michael at the Israel Museum made an appointment for us at eleven o'clock this morning,"

"Our witching hour time to meet priests," I said.

"So, let's go downstairs and fortify ourselves with some hearty Ukrainian breakfast and get going. We can talk about what Zosia said last night. A hidden cousin. Maybe the priest would have some information on that."

Kasha, porridge made from buckwheat, was about the most appealing item on the menu, though the server looked offended when I carefully plucked off the pork rinds that floated decorously on top. I also treated myself to something sweet—an order of fruit and apple-filled varenyky—though these too-doughy dumplings landed both onto my plate and into my stomach like small lead balloons. Simon cleaned his plate of Ukrainian hash, a conglomeration of eggs, potatoes, onions, and chunks of bulbous greasy sausage. A large pot of tea gave us some relief from the draftiness that seeped through the vintage windowpanes in the hotel dining room.

"Well," I said as I poured myself a third cup, "The food's not that important. And we did just come from Rome."

"A gourmet experience is definitely not why we're here," he said. "Back to Zosia. I gather she sort of blew you off last night."

"Not really. It's probably painful for her, since she has found no one, but she did give me the original Berkowski clue. Maybe Esther Berkowski Weinberg and her husband Chaim were my aunt and uncle. Even if they ran a branch of the Berkowski business here mainly selling Judaica, no local gallery owners now would know about it. Or admit to knowing."

"If there are even any dealers, Jewish or non, alive from that time," said Simon. "But remember in Shanghai, when we were looking for the Torah Ruth's aunt and uncle had stolen, there was old Mr. Xu in the antiques market. He was pretty much of an antique himself but he turned out to be very helpful, because he had known the original owners of the Torah from the Jewish community there before the war."

"Yes," I said, "helpful until he was murdered. I still think Father Stash's death is not a coincidence either. Like Avi's mother Helen Wolf in London, who died when I was looking for the looted Seder plate. Ruth being nearly killed on the street in Shanghai. And us being almost run over in the Vatican. Do we really want to get ourselves entangled with such dangerous crooks again?"

"You surprise me, Lily; of the two of us you've always been the one to persevere, no matter what."

"Maybe this Jewish Miss Marple thing is wearing thin. More likely, it's being here in Lviv. This brings back such a basically ugly memory of my father and his family and of the nature of my parents' relationship in general. Despite what a jerk he really was, and how busy he was, he was very attentive to me and indulgent, and my mother was stricter. Later—too late—I came to realize how much she loved me. My childhood is like a scab that has healed over but opens up again with just a little scrape against something sharp."

Simon took my hand across the stained tablecloth.

"I know, but looking for The Duck is what I've been sent here to do. Yes, he's probably dangerous, but I'm trained in ways you don't even know about. Plus, we never know when a trusty colleague will show up. You've done amazingly well in the tough spots, Lily, but I feel badly that this time it's an assignment for me that coincidentally dredged up your past. I shouldn't have dragged you here. I just count on your good sense and crave your companionship. But I don't want you to be in pain."

"It's not your fault. In fact, if you remember, Judaica emerging from the Iron Curtain was *my* original magazine assignment when I met you. I never got to that. If I sniff something out, I'm sure my editor Marty will be only too happy to finally get the story. Unfortunately, the minor clue I have now won't help either of us. But your hunt for The Duck and the codex is the main priority."

We finished breakfast and bundled up. The greyness made the streets and sidewalks, dotted with patches of ice and snow, look grimy.

Litter scattered around did not help. Most people walked with their heads down to avoid these hazards. And eye contact with strangers. However, a few women wearing raggedy furs stared at the bulky but cozy black hooded down coat in which I routinely trudged around New York City.

We circled around the adorned column that memorializes Adam Mickewicz, Lviv's native son patriot poet who championed Ukrainian independence in the nineteenth century. At Ploshcha Rynok (Market Square) ice skaters whirled around a rink surrounded on four sides by wooden houses. A row of food and souvenir vendors lined up outside the rink, the seasonal Christmas market.

"It is pretty," I said. "Though not exactly Rockefeller Center. Where's the big tree? And where are we going?"

"To the Arch Cathedral Basilica of the Assumption of the Blessed Virgin Mary," said Simon.

"Wow, that's a mouthful."

"An eyeful, too. Look. It's that long, narrow grey stone building. They call it the Latin Cathedral for short. And we're supposed to be greeted at the main entrance by one Father Kazimierz Dabrowski. That must be him, the guy hovering in the doorway without an over-coat."

This priest was about six-feet-tall and lean, probably the most fit person, male or female, I had seen since we arrived in Lviv, unless the voluminous coats disguised some decent shapes. Father Dabrowski wore just the plain, everyday garb of a contemporary priest anywhere: black suit, white clerical collar. That he was surprisingly young I deemed a negative for the purpose of digging up the Jewish past. Also, he was probably a peon on the bureaucratic ladder, just the unlucky one assigned to meet with some pesky Jews sent here by the Israel Museum.

After introductions and everyone's insistence we use first names— we were to call him Kaz—he gave us a short tour of the basilica first built in the fourteenth century. The altar area was beautifully outfitted with gold walls and statuary and crystal chandeliers. I wondered out loud if the cathedral had been reopened or restored since the end of the Soviet Union.

"Spruced up a bit," Father Kaz said, "but it and one other church here in Lviv remained physically open and accessible the whole time under the Soviets. The priests, however, were confined to a small town near the Polish border until His Holiness Pope John Paul blessed us four years ago by reactivating the diocese. You know there's also a Ukrainian Catholic branch akin to the Eastern Orthodox denominations. Here in Lviv we on the Roman side represent more the history and traditions of our ethnic Poles."

"Very beautiful," I said. "But, Father, how did you even become a priest? Surely, there were not operating seminaries for many, many years. You weren't even born before 1945."

He laughed and pointed our way back up the main aisle and out of the basilica toward a nondescript building behind the cathedral. He led us into a small room with faded paint on the walls, a broken linoleum floor, a sink, refrigerator, and microwave. While Simon and I sat down around a small round table, Kaz filled a large measuring cup with water, which he heated in the microwave and divided into three mugs loaded with tea bags. He brought ours to the table, got his own, and sat down.

"You asked about my education as a priest. You're right, of course, that wasn't feasible under the Soviets. However, I was fortunate enough to be sent to Rome to the Pontifical Gregorian University. It was founded by the Jesuits. They were prominent in our church here for many centuries. I followed the honorable path of many young men from this city in studying there when I went to Rome fifteen years ago. By that time the election of the Polish pope had given hope to many Catholics in the Soviet-controlled countries. Hope for a return to religion along with the movement toward independence. One of the arguments Lech Walesa used in fighting for independence in Poland was to point out the atheism of the Communist way had not helped us, but returning to belief in God would be beneficial. I guess you would say my parents and I bought into that argument."

"We met another priest from here, many years older than you, in Rome last week," Simon said. "Father Stash Gajos. He was in Rome for a long time. Since the war."

Father Kaz looked somewhat flustered before he answered.

"I know of him. By repute. We never met."

"Have you heard that he died in the past few days?"

Now he turned truly ashen.

"No, I hadn't heard," he said. "He was not a young man. Some illness overtook him, I presume."

"Maybe a heart attack," I said. "It was very sudden, however. Lively one day and gone the next."

"A pity, but it happens." He seemed eager to change the subject.

"I'm honored that so august an institution as the Israel Museum has sent you to see our church. I traveled to Israel two years ago and I very much enjoyed spending time in that museum. I bring regrets from the Archbishop, who himself has left for his own pilgrimage. Not to the Holy Land, I'm afraid, just to visit relatives in Chicago for the Christmas holidays. I know he will be most distressed to hear the news about Father Stash. They were boyhood friends. So, what brings you here?"

"Father Stash had in his possession a codex of The TaZ. Do you know who that was? The TaZ?" Simon asked.

"Indeed I do. Rabbi David Ha-Levi Segal. The scholar who prayed and presided at the synagogue sentimentally, if wrong-headedly, later called the Golden Rose. There was a time when that place was called The TaZ Synagogue to commemorate his great commentary, *Turei Zahav*. A better name, I dare say, than Golden Rose. Her sacrifice, if the story is true, is a blemish on both the Jews and the Jesuits."

"I don't know enough about the story," I said. "Why do you say that?"

Father Kaz said, "The legend goes that her husband's family built the synagogue on land that the Jesuits contended was theirs and later sued, or whatever the process was in those days, to take over the building and its site. The daughter-in-law, the proverbial Golden Rose, went as emissary to negotiate with the Jesuits, possibly bearing a bribe from the family to persuade the priests to give up the dispute. She was never seen or heard from again. As I said, so the legend goes. But the synagogue remained in the hands of the Jews."

"Until the Nazis," I said.

He nodded.

"A codex of writings of The TaZ?" he asked. "So a version of his famous commentary or something else?"

"A sheaf of papers bound in leather that seem to have been written by hand during his lifetime," said Simon. "I didn't have enough time to read much of the contents, but it seemed to be personal reflections. It was not formatted like Talmudic commentary. Also, I could tell it was a palimpsest."

"A palimpsest? I'm afraid I don't know what that is. I'm more of a pastoral priest than a super scholar."

"A document that is written over something else where there has been an effort to erase what's underneath either to cover it up or simply to save paper."

"How interesting," Kaz said. "I need to put this all together. You are here representing the Israel Museum. Father Stash, a native son of Lviv with a long career of service at the Vatican, had in his possession a work of a Jewish scholar who was the leader of this city's most beautiful historic synagogue. I'm afraid I don't follow."

Simon and I laughed. It did sound ridiculous. This young priest was pretty sharp. And we were impressed by his knowledge of The TaZ and the Golden Rose.

"I agree," said Simon. "It all sounds far-fetched. Preposterous even. Father Stash contacted the Israel Museum with a proposal to sell the codex to the museum. The museum contacted me—some call me an expert on Jewish manuscripts and books of certain vintages—to go to

Rome to see what he had. Which Lily and I did. Father Stash showed us the codex, which he had secured in what he thought was a safe, if temporary, place. The next day we had another meeting scheduled, and he was to introduce us to the person who had brought him the codex. A priest named Kaczka, whom Father Stash referred to as The Duck."

"Ha," said Father Kaz. "Yes, I get the Polish joke. And did you meet this priest?"

"No, when we returned to Father Stash's apartment, we learned from his housekeeper that he had died during the night. We immediately went to the location where the codex had been stored and heard it had vanished just as surely as Father Stash himself."

"Oh, my, what a set of circumstances. That Father Stash . . ."

"What about him?" I sensed Father Kaz spoke from prior knowledge.

"Well, it is not good to speak ill of the dead. But I will only say his reputation among younger priests wasn't the finest. Not that he did anything wrong that affected us personally. Just a few people's parents remembered him from the old days. He was in Rome a very long time. Even before the Nazis and the Iron Curtain. Those were turbulent times in European history and politics in which the Vatican sometimes played a role behind the scenes."

What was he getting at? Politics, history, the Vatican. I ventured a guess.

"Are you telling us Father Stash was involved in the ratlines? Funneling Nazis out of Europe after the war?"

"There were rumors."

"What you're telling us, if the rumors had any validity," I said, "might help us make some sense of this whole thing."

Simon gave me a smile that said the Jewish Miss Marple is back. Father Kaz looked perplexed.

"What do you mean?"

"Remember, Simon, even when you first got the call from the Israel Museum, you were surprised the Vatican itself wouldn't keep the codex, if it were so authentic and valuable? And then, when we got to Rome, we were surprised we weren't meeting with Father Stash in the Vatican Museum or some other official place. We started at his apartment and went with him to the trattoria next door, owned by his friend Franco, and that's where he had stored the codex. The whole thing was fishy, to say the least. And the next day, when we found out Father Stash was dead, the housekeeper said The Duck had visited the night before. We went over to the restaurant and Franco told us The Duck had been there and took the codex after asking for an expensive bottle of wine and sending Franco down to his cellar to get it."

"I don't follow," said Kaz. "What does this have to do with the ratline rumors?"

"I'm not one hundred percent sure," I said, "but the codex was obviously looted from either a Jewish institution or a private collection."

"But how did The Duck come by it? And how did he know Father Stash?" Kaz asked.

"Father Stash said there were some old connections between his family here and The Duck's," said Simon. "The codex was supposedly among the belongings of The Duck's deceased mother, which is a pretty suspicious story, don't you think?"

"Agreed," said Kaz. "So ratline rumors, Nazi-looted art, that's the thread you're pulling here, right?"

I nodded.

"Kaz, do you know this Kaczka, or anything about him?" I asked.

"I do not. I'm acquainted with all the currently active priests in Lviv and I've never heard of him. If he's of Stash's era, or even somewhat younger, he could have given up the active priesthood during the Communist years. Let me ask you this, was or is the Israel Museum prepared to buy the codex?"

"No," Simon said, "for one thing the museum doesn't buy work lacking provenance. Not knowingly, at least . . ."

"There have been cases?"

"Unfortunately, yes. But this wouldn't be one of them. It absolutely reeks of treachery. And clouded provenance could be only one of the criminal issues. Lily suspects The Duck had something to do with Father Stash's death."

Kaz looked genuinely shocked.

"I'd like to help," he said. "One thing I can do is talk to my Jesuit friends about the Father Stash rumors. And maybe see if I can find anything in diocese files on a Father Kaczka, perhaps student records. Between the Germans and the Soviets, however, there aren't many."

"Do you know any identified Jews here?"

"Lily, there is a woman professor at the Lviv Academy of the Arts who organized an exhibition of Jewish art five years ago at the Museum of Ethnography and Art Crafts in Lviv. I went; I might even have the program from it . . ."

He got up, reached for a pile of pamphlets on a shelf above the microwave, plopped it onto the table, and rifled through it.

"Ah, here it is."

"Traditional Jewish Art of the 17th-early 20th Century" was the title of the exhibit. A business card was clipped to the program booklet.

"Doctor Faina Petryakova. We will call her," I said. "Can we keep this, Kaz?"

The priest got up again and held out his hand.

"Of course. Please let me know how your quest goes, and I will try to figure out any other way I can help."

Outdoors again, we were relieved to see sunshine brightening up the frozen landscape.

"Maybe the sun is a good omen, a sign we're making progress," I said.

"Ever the optimist," Simon said, kissing my forehead. "I'm glad to see your good spirits are returning. Maybe Father Kaz has put us on to a couple of leads. Between the information about Father Stash and this woman professor of arts. From the title it looked like her exhibit time line encompassed the working life of The TaZ. Maybe she knows something about the codex. That program really isn't a catalogue that says anything about specific pieces. But wouldn't it be amazing if the codex was even in the exhibit? I wonder where she got *whatever* was in the exhibit. How much of it was looted art, considering how long it was since there was active Jewish life in the USSR."

"Whether there was looted art in the exhibit or not," I said, "if the codex was on display, it would mean The Duck or someone else stole it again since 1990. That might be easier to trace than going all the way back to before the war."

By this time we had walked to the site of the Golden Rose synagogue. Where a sizeable compound of designated spaces for worship, study, and ritual bath had once thrived what remained visible was one sandstone wall fronted by rubble and barren tree branches. A gunmetal plaque framed in red brick explained in Ukrainian and English that this was built by the Nachmanowicz family between 1550 and 1595 in memory of the founder's wife and destroyed by the Nazis in 1942. And it was called in Yiddish *Di Goldene Royz*.

"But Father Kaz's version of the legend had it that the Golden Rose who saved the building was a daughter-in-law," said Simon.

"That must have been after it was built," I said, "and the wife must have died sooner."

"It's probably not critical that you and I are clear on this detail," he said. "In the total scope of the history here and what we're doing, it probably doesn't matter. Besides, it is just legend, according to Kaz."

"You didn't get much chance to read the codex," I said. "Did you ever think it might relate to this place or the legend? Wasn't The TaZ the rabbi here?"

"Indeed. You might be right. We should only be so lucky as to get the opportunity to find out what he wrote."

"Let's walk back toward the hotel," I said. "I've had it, and it's so cold out. We can try to reach that arts professor. I don't know what else we can accomplish today."

"Well, I could sure use a nap," Simon said, using our code for making love in the afternoon. He took my arm to escort me off the rubble and back onto the cobble stone street. We walked back toward the Rynok Square and passed by the Italianate courtyard of the Lviv Historical Museum, a complex of several adjacent buildings. In the main Korniakt House I saw a sign: Gothic Hall Antique and Modern Art Shop.

"Let's just go in here for a moment," I said.

"I bet we will be in here for longer than a moment, but that's fine. Whatever you want," said Simon.

"You like to peruse antique stores more than I do," I said.

"Guilty as charged."

The store was indeed Gothic, but the assortment displayed ranged from trinkets to jewelry to furniture to paintings. I knew what I was looking for, but it wasn't there. Simon, as a diamond and fine jewelry dealer, moved among the cases of vintage and antique pieces quickly, stopping only once or twice when something caught his trained eye.

"That's a good one," he said, pointing to a platinum and diamond brooch. "Art Deco, Paris 1931, Cartier, I think. I wonder what it's doing here and whose it was. See anything you like?"

"I'm not looking to buy," I said. "Let's move on."

Crossing another small square toward our hotel we came upon a shop where an oil painting labeled in English as "Market in the Galician Town" was propped up on an easel in the window.

"Doesn't this sort of look like Kozakiewicz? Let's go in," I said.

A pleasant-looking middle-aged woman, wearing the universal gallery-keeper attire of black pants and black sweater, emerged from a door in the back of a gallery space no larger than our hotel room. Metal glasses hung from a cord around her neck. The shoe polish black color of her hair, cut helmet-style, matched her eye makeup. All in all the look of a wannabe younger woman running a modern art gallery. She was very solicitous as she introduced herself as Halina and asked if we were looking for anything in particular.

"I really like the work of A. Kozakiewicz," I said. "Isn't that one of his in the window?"

"Indeed it, is, madame. Let me take it down for you," she said as she reached up a slight platform, lifted the easel down, and turned it around to face into the room.

"This is a little pale and muted," I said. "I've seen some with richer, deeper colors and more pastoral. There's one with a mother and her children feeding sticks into an outdoor fire."

"I've never seen that one, but someone else recently mentioned such a scene to me," she said.

"Really? Is it unusual for you to be asked about the same sort of painting?"

"Well, you know Kozakiewicz is not exactly Rembrandt or Picasso . . ."

I couldn't resist.

"You mean someone in Lviv might be looking for a Rembrandt or Picasso?"

"You'd be surprised how people here are starting to make money. Of course, people like that can go to Paris or New York. Still, it's unfortunate how rare it is to find someone here who appreciates Polish painters of the last century."

"Perhaps the other person who inquired is someone looking to determine the value of a painting in his possession," said Simon.

"No, it was nothing like that, sir. And it wasn't a gentleman, anyway. It was a woman, one of our most esteemed medical doctors. I was honored to have her come into my gallery. Dr. Zubko of the gynecological hospital. She was walking by, like you, and came in when she saw this one. She said her grandparents had a similar painting, and seeing this and the painter's name Kozakiewicz gave her a pleasant sense of nostalgia for old times."

"Such a coincidence," said Simon, "two women asking about a similar painting. Her grandparents owned one, she told you? How old is this woman?"

"Oh, Dr. Zubko, has been a prominent doctor for many years. I think she must be about seventy years old. She's a little round but very pretty and her hair is still blonde with only a little grey mixed in. Though at her age she would look better if she put in a little color."

God knows, Halina was an expert in hair color.

"You know, we're just visiting. But, if this doctor is so good, maybe I should go in for a consultation," I said. "Do you have her card and phone number?"

It was a long shot, I knew, but Halina was shooting off her mouth sufficiently to give me the opening and the chutzpah to ask.

"Oh, I would never violate the confidence of a client and give out her contact information. I mean, she is not a client yet, but one can always hope."

Simon and I looked at each other and could barely contain ourselves.

"Never mind," I said. "I will manage. Thank you for your time."

Outside, giving each other high fives and a big hug in full view of the oh-so-discreet Halina, we had no idea what she thought and could not have cared less.

"A good day's work, Miss Marple," said Simon. "And now let's go back to the hotel for that nap."

"With these new leads," I said. "we do have some calls to make."

"They can wait."

Three hours later the telephone in our room jangled us both out of deep sleep—the real, restful nap that followed a profound mutual physical release of pent-up tension. Muttering "damn," Simon groped for the phone next to him.

"Yes? . . . Who is this?"

He hung up.

"A crank call. Forget it. Look, it's five-thirty already. What a great afternoon."

"Simon, don't give me that crank call bit. Who was it? What did they say?"

"It was a man who said 'if you think Lviv is cold now, wait 'til you die here.'"

"Well, that was succinct and clear. Do we think this was The Duck?"

"I suppose," Simon said. "Just when we got you so relaxed . . ."

"Yes, but you know a little threat has never stopped me, or us, before. Nor did a murder along the way. You know what? It's too late to try to call either the arts professor or the gynecologist, so let's get up and go out on the town for a nice dinner in Lviv and forget about The Duck."

Chapter 14

The next morning at nine-fifteen Simon called the office of Professor Faina Petryakova. We decided he should call because of the expertise in rare Jewish scholarly works that made him the Mossad's go-to guy when a case involving one arose. Although it was a passionate hobby and not an academic career, he had developed something of a reputation in this scholarly field even with no public connection to his part-time employer.

Once he reached the professor's office, his eye rolling and responses told me he was frustrated with the answers coming from the other side of the conversation.

"Is she traveling or at home? . . . But are you in contact with the professor? Is it possible for me to leave her a message? . . . Thank you. Would you tell her that Mr. Simon Rieger of New York City called? I'm visiting in Lviv for the next few days. I'm calling to inquire about the pieces that were displayed in the 1990 exhibition of Jewish art. I'm staying at the George Hotel. If she can call me here, I would appreciate it . . . Yes. Thank you very much. Goodbye."

"So," I said, "what's up? Where is she?"

"I have no idea," Simon said. "Her assistant sounded about as friendly as a female concentration camp guard. Tough. The professor is on leave until after the first of January."

"That's still three weeks away. I heard you ask if she's home or traveling. What did the assistant say?"

"She wouldn't. She took the message, and maybe we will hear from her. Maybe we won't. We have to move on. Now it's your turn on the telephone."

"I'm going to get the number of the gynecological hospital. I wonder if there's a phone book here anywhere."

I pulled out all the drawers in the scratched faux Baroque bedside tables and dresser to no avail. But I found one on a shelf in the closet. The only thing on the cover I could understand was the number 1992. It was all written with Cyrillic letters.

"Let's go down to breakfast and bribe the concierge to give us the phone number of the hospital."

Simon laughed.

"You think that's what it will take?"

"Well, a nice tip."

Back in the room fifty minutes later, stoked by another hearty morning meal and relieved of five US dollars, I dialed the number and asked to be connected to the office of Dr. Zubko. The assistant who answered sounded every bit as brusque and impatient as Simon had described Professor Petryakova's. I wondered if telephone rudeness was listed as a requisite skill on job descriptions.

When I asked to speak with the doctor, the assistant told me she did not take calls from people she did not know.

"Okay, well, can I make an appointment?"

"How old are you?"

"In my sixties," I said.

"And you have a gynecological issue?"

I hesitated because it had been a while. I had to think up something relevant.

"Well, I still have hot flashes, but I'm also concerned about my daughter."

"Hot flashes. Big deal. What's your daughter's problem? Why can't she make an appointment?"

"I would rather not say. I'd like to see the doctor."

"Okay. Can you pay the fee?"

"How much?"

"You're not from here. American? British?"

"Actually, both."

"You can come tomorrow ten o'clock in the morning. It will be one hundred dollars US."

"Thank you very much."

I got off and gave Simon a relieved thumbs up.

"Whew. Forget concentration camps. These assistants could work for the Mossad."

"Nah," he said. "Most of ours have more charm. When they choose to apply it. She put you through the wringer. But you got an appointment. When? Oh, and how much?"

"Ten o'clock tomorrow morning and one hundred dollars. And worth every penny and more, if this good Dr. Zubko had grandparents with an ugly Kozakiewicz painting . . ."

"And maybe, just maybe, might be your missing cousin. I'm so happy and excited for you. How do you feel about this?"

"Optimistic but cautiously so. Definitely not as depressed about being here as I was, that's for sure."

"That's enough for me. What shall we do today? Back to the museum area to see more than the store? Look for any landmarks of the Jewish community? Memorials?"

"Ugh," I said. "Sight-seeing in the graveyard countries. Maybe the museum. It looked like a whole complex of several buildings clustered together. I guess that's a good way to pass several hours. I just wish . . ."

"What?"

"That we could make as much progress on finding the codex as we may have made on finding out about my family. After all, the codex is the reason we came here in the first place."

"I'm not worried," he said. "I had the feeling from my conversation with Professor Faina's assistant that her boss was within reach. Maybe I will hear from her."

"The sooner, the better," I said. "We don't want the Mossad to cut off your expense account that's keeping us in the style to which we're accustomed, including in this luxury hotel."

"Right. Good thing I still have my day job. For so many reasons."

We put on our coats and went downstairs to leave the hotel when the front desk clerk, phone receiver in hand, called out.

"Mr. Rieger? Aren't you Mr. Rieger? You have a phone call."

"Maybe we're saved by the bell just in the nick of time," I said, moving back with him away from the entrance, where I was already shivering before we even went outside.

"Yes, this is Simon Rieger," he said listing onto the counter, because the receiver was still held by the clerk's outstretched hand. "Thank you for returning my call. Yes, that would be very nice. I will take that down and we will speak then."

He leaned away for the instant it took for him to reach into his coat pocket and withdraw a small black notebook with pen attached. He tried to write as far away from the clerk's range of vision as possible.

"Yes, got it. Thank you very much."

Simon nodded to the clerk indicating he could hang up the phone. He signaled to me that we should go back upstairs.

"I hope that was the professor," I said when we got there. "Why did we need to come up again?"

"I am calling her back. On my mobile. She is at home, and gave me the number."

"Great. At least the bitchy assistant gave her the message."

"Yes, . . . oh, hello again, Professor Petryakova. Thank you so much for returning my call . . . yes, yes, Lviv is very nice. A little cold, but interesting. Professor, I understand you're on leave from the university but, if you're in the city in the next few days, I would really appreciate the opportunity to meet with you . . . all right . . . that would be nice. And the address? Just a moment, let me get my pen . . ."

He pointed to his coat, which he had just offloaded onto the bed, and I retrieved the notebook and handed it to him. He made a notation, thanked the professor, and ended the call.

"We're going to her home at three-thirty this afternoon. We might as well stick with our original plan, go to the museum, and then to her house."

Touring the Lviv Historical Museum, housed in a former royal residence, took us through four floors of baroque rooms randomly filled with artifacts labeled in the Cyrillic alphabet. It passed the time, which was the chief reason we visited in the first place. After a couple of boring hours we returned outside, where the temperature seemed the least blustery since our arrival. Not that it was balmy enough to even consider shedding any of our winter accessories, but at least it was more comfortable to stroll around until our meeting with Professor Petryakova.

On another corner of the endlessly diverse Rynok Square we came across a building with the implausible sign Pharmacy Under the Black Eagle, the Pharmacy Museum. Housed in an old drugstore opened by a military pharmacist in 1735 and still operating as a working pharmacy, it displayed medical instruments and appliances, prescriptions, medicine bottles, an ancient pill-making device, and an impressive eighteenth century scale decorated with meter-high figures of the God of Medical Treatment and his daughter, the Goddess of Health. There was a library jammed with pharmaceutical books. One room told the history of pharmacy, and another was a reconstructed laboratory.

"Now, this is what I would call a fun museum," Simon said. "Much more interesting than the history one."

By the time we finished in there it was three-ten.

"We need to find a cab to go to the Professor's house," Simon said. "She said it was about a five- or ten- minute drive from the center. I don't see any. Let's go back into the drugstore and ask a pharmacist to call one."

We returned to the store part of the building and saw a stooped man with a shock of white hair that matched his walrus mustache painfully reaching to grab a brown overcoat from a wall hook before exchanging it for the lab coat he had just taken off. He looked as if he had worked there since the store opened.

"Excuse me," Simon said, "but is it possible to call a taxi for us to get to this address?"

When the man looked at the notebook page, he said, "No need for a taxi. I will take you in my car. I live very near there. The next street."

Simon and I looked at each other. This was the friendliest stranger we had encountered in Lviv. It seemed safe to accept his offer. Except . . . he still drove? Did we trust him on the road? We shrugged and figured okay. It was supposed to be a short trip.

We walked a half block to a narrow alley where a tiny, rusted, olive green two-door Lada was parked. Our erstwhile chauffeur, who had introduced himself as Leonid, opened the front passenger door, flipped up the seat back, and pointed to me. I curled into the back. Simon, who is not really tall, folded himself into the front head first before Leonid banged the door shut and went around to the driver's seat and started the car. The engine coughed into action and jolted forward when Leonid jerked the manual shift lever.

"You are Americans," he said while accelerating to career us into the main street as if the Lada could win the Indy 500, "here for tourism in winter? You must be crazy. Crazy Americans, we always say. But welcome."

"Thank you, thank you," Simon said, gripping the dashboard that touched his knees crouched roughly up to his stomach. "This is only a short drive, right?"

"Ha, ha! Are you nervous about my driving? It's okay. I have never had an accident in the seventy-nine years I have been driving."

I quickly calculated that, if he got a license at sixteen, Leonid was now ninety-five. But sixteen and a license were civilized western thinking.

"Yes, started by driving truck for my father's grocery store," he said. "Only eleven years old. Still driving almost eighty years later."

So, only ninety-one. Leonid surely had seen a lot in his lifetime, and I was curious to know more about him. But there was no way I wanted to distract him from the road so I deliberately refrained from asking any questions. Simon also stayed uncharacteristically silent. No matter. Leonid's monologue throughout the trip answered some without any prompting.

"Always lived in Lviv. Lemberg, Lwów. Lived through them all. The names. The Empire. The Poles, the Nazis, the Russians. Someone always coming through and staying long enough to kill off some Ukrainians. But we're pretty good at killing each other, too, especially killing the Jews. No need for Hitler's permission. Yes, people here could have taken care of every one of them. And would have."

This ride had taken an uncomfortable turn that almost made me forget the perilous driving. Did Leonid size us up to be Jewish? Which side was he on? What would come next? Could we believe anything he said?

"Me, though, I liked the Jews. Matter of fact, a Jewish man paid for me to go to pharmacy school. Old Mr. Spekulant. Fine gentleman, he was, from Radom. Moved here and ran his jewelry business. Good customer of my father. Saw my potential, you would say. Asked me what I wanted to do and paid my way. I really would have liked to be a medical doctor but I didn't want to ask for so much. Smart man, Mr. Spekulant, moved away to America before the Nazis. I don't imagine you know him."

"America is a big place," said Simon.

"Of course. I know that. One thing helpful about working in a pharmacy. I know a lot of doctors personally. I'm the only pharmacist they trust. Many I even knew when they were young and worked with me while they were getting through school. Some of them have retired or died, but, me, I'm still going strong."

He stopped short in front of a prewar four-story apartment building hung on each level with balconies edged with wrought-iron railings.

Simon and I unrolled ourselves out of the car, grateful we could stand up straight again. Leonid got out and came over to say goodbye.

"Thank you so much," I said.

"If it's not insulting to you, I'd be happy to offer you something for your gas and service," said Simon, reaching for his pocket. "We appreciate your bringing us here but we had planned to take a taxi and . . ."

Leonid held us his hand and said, "Sure. I'm not insulted. How about ten dollars US?"

"Certainly," Simon said and handed over a ten-dollar bill.

Walking to the entrance to the building, we both laughed.

"It was worth the ten just to have arrived in one piece," I said.

"More," said Simon.

Chapter 15

Professor Faina Petryakova opened the door of her apartment on the second floor. Though she appeared to be a woman of sixty-something like me, we could tell she had been a beauty in her day. She retained an exquisitely smooth face and erect posture, topped by a tightly upswept hairdo pinned with a small gold and sapphire clip. Resplendent in a royal blue silk caftan, she greeted us each with an individual embrace as if we were old friends rather than just getting introduced.

She led us into a sitting room that was simply furnished with Danish modern chairs and sofa, but they were the only minimalist elements of decor. The simple seating flanked a massive oval glass coffee table bearing on each end a round silver tray that held, respectively, silver Kiddush cups and spice boxes used for the Havdalah ritual that closes Shabbat. In the middle was another tray laden with a silver tea service, three china cups and saucers, and a tiered glass epergne that held dainty tea sandwiches and pastries. From where we sat we could see a small dining room dominated by a glass-fronted cabinet crammed with pieces of silver Judaica of varying sizes and functions: a Torah crown and several Torah finials, Seder plates, mezuzas, and menorahs. Massive silver candlesticks dominated a round Danish dining table. On the few open areas of wall space not occupied by overflowing bookcases were interspersed black-and-white lithographs and woodcuts in the style of the German Expressionists Hitler disparaged as degenerate.

I was taken aback by the plethora of aesthetic Judaism in this city which had gladly disposed of most of its Jews and where I felt— justifiably or not—the lingering hostility to be palpable. I could see

Simon, much more knowledgeable in this genre than I, was equally impressed.

"You are quite a Judaica collector, Madame Professor," he said. "Beautiful, beautiful pieces. And, if I might say, surprising to find here and now."

She smiled and began to pour tea.

"First off," she said, "it's Faina, and I hope I can call you Lily and Simon."

"Of course," we said in unison.

"I am still an oddity here in Lviv, being so open about my Jewish identity, but maybe I've been tolerated because I'm not a native. I am from the place now known as Belarus. I came to Lviv to get my doctorate and stayed to work here. This is a time of hope in the former Soviet countries, hope for revival of our many diverse ethnic cultures to be shared and celebrated. Certainly that has been my dream and my goal throughout my career."

"The exhibit you organized five years ago was a bold step toward achieving that goal," said Simon. "Very impressive."

"Thank you. It was a first step that was well received. Much of what you see here in my home was in the exhibit. I have gathered these items during my travels and through friends; many pieces are from Jewish communities that do not even exist anymore."

I glanced at Simon and could tell we were thinking the same thing: where and how did she get all this? Tempting as it was, questioning the professor on the provenance of her collection was not our mission. I helped myself to a cucumber tea sandwich and sipped my tea.

Faina said, "It's an unexpected pleasure to welcome guests from the US, especially guests so connected to Judaism, and, you, Simon, a scholar on texts. Do tell me what brings you to Lviv and what I can do to help you enjoy your trip."

"Faina," Simon said, "it is an honor to meet you and we are very grateful to be here in your home and while you are on leave, according to your assistant."

"Oh, that," she said, "I had a minor medical procedure the other day. That's all. Since the Christmas holidays at the university begin next week, it was a good opportunity to take off extra time to get some research done with no administrative duties to interrupt me. My students were only too happy to have one extra week without class to study for mid-year examinations."

"I trust you are healing well and recovering from your procedure," I said.

"Oh, yes, it was just a minor female thing. Now, tell me, why did you want to meet?"

"I assume you know of The TaZ, . . ." said Simon.

"Of course, probably the most famous rabbi and scholar of this city."

"I'm wondering if you have ever seen or heard of a codex The TaZ either personally wrote or dictated during his lifetime, as opposed to the commentaries that were published later. I have recently seen this codex in Rome but I believe it has returned to Lviv and thought you might know where to find it."

Faina looked genuinely shocked.

"A codex of The TaZ? Oh, my! I have never seen one but have heard there were many rare treasures in the archives of his synagogue . . ."

"The Golden Rose," I said.

"Yes, the Golden Rose is one name, but it's also referred to as The TaZ synagogue for its famous rabbi."

"So," said Simon, "this codex was not included in your exhibit in 1990?"

"Absolutely not. It would be a thrill just to see such a text, believe me. How did it get to Rome?"

"It was brought there by a priest called Father Kaczka. We call him The Duck."

"Yes, The Duck, in Polish," said Faina. "Have you tried to find this Duck through the church?"

"Yes," I said. "In fact, at the church we met a young priest called Father Kaz who suggested we meet you."

"Aha. I wondered. I believe I have met the young priest. Unfortunately, as I didn't even know of the existence of this codex, never mind of The Duck, I cannot help you. But please have more sandwiches and some cake."

"You mentioned your medical procedure," I said. "Was it performed at the gynecological hospital?"

"Yes, of course. That is the premiere medical facility for women. Did you know it was the Jewish Hospital before the war? In addition to its excellent care, it's a remarkable building. Moorish architecture, a beautiful dome, gorgeous tiles. The setting is also imposing—high on a slope with a lovely view. Worthwhile to visit, even if you're not a patient, which I would hope you will not be."

"It sounds interesting. As it happens, I did arrange a consultation tomorrow with a Dr. Zubko? Would you happen to know her?"

"Only by reputation. She is a hero among women here for helping those who are raped or molested or physically abused by men. Unfortunately, her work with these women is almost an underground operation, because this is not a cause that gets much support from other doctors or the police or judges. We live in an old-fashioned place with the mind set to match: men believe they have leeway to treat women however they want, and women who are victims are thought to have brought violent acts onto themselves. Very sad and unenlightened. However, my reading and my travels convince me that such attitudes make life challenging for women even in countries such as yours that claim to be more equal and progressive. Would you agree?"

"Reluctantly, yes," I said. "It is still a man's world in every aspect, but I would like to think women are catching up professionally, at least, though they're often held to higher standards in terms of qualifications, performance, and, of course, balancing work and family responsibilities. Violence against women—oh, my, where do I start? That festers like a petri dish of germs fed by upbringing, cultural norms, an inherently violent nature . . ."

"Whew," said Simon. "Strong stuff, Lily. Good thing you don't lump me into such a rotten cesspool of male species."

"Hardly," I said. "But Faina, how does Dr. Zubko manage to do this work, if the medical establishment doesn't support her in it?"

"I have heard there is a small network of private homes offered by caring people. In these homes Dr. Zubko directs the installation of hygienic examination and laboratory spaces where she and a very few other doctors and nurses go as volunteers when they are off-duty. One of the houses is quite large and functions as a temporary shelter for women who need to leave home."

"And how do women who need these services find out where to go?"

"Word of mouth, a rare sympathetic priest or lawyer or policeman. Unfortunately, the need is greater than what Dr. Zubko and her cohort can take care of. She is a pioneer."

"And she does this in addition to her busy schedule at the hospital?"

"Yes. In a way her position at the hospital provides her some cover for this other work. And it protects her from any trouble from the authorities for running uncertified clinics. No one would touch Dr. Zubko. She is beloved by patients and colleagues for her medical skills and compassion. And her husband is a judge. That certainly helps, too."

"Are you friends? Have you known her for a long time?"

"No, not friends, but we are acquainted. We meet at events such as government receptions. At one of these she specifically mentioned to me having seen the exhibit on Jewish art. But we have never had any one-to-one social connection or even a private conversation. Which is a pity, as I suspect she is a very engaging and interesting person."

"Is it possible she's Jewish, too?"

My question obviously startled Faina. She hesitated before answering, evidently determined to give a thoughtful response.

"No," she said deliberately. "I have absolutely never heard even a whisper about Dr. Zubko being a Jew. And one does hear rumors like that, especially now that it's somewhat more acceptable to find one's Jewish roots and acknowledge that identity. But, Dr. Zubko, no. With her long career and stellar reputation at the hospital and her husband's rank all these years, I can't imagine anything like that. As I told you when you arrived, I am truly an exception to be openly Jewish and to hold a prestigious academic position all these years. Even the people now accepting that they or their families are Jewish are already at least a generation removed and have no notion of what Judaism is. As an educator also educated about the Jewish religion and culture, I am truly an anomaly in this country."

"And also a pioneer," I said.

"Yes, that, too. A pioneer within a five thousand-year-old people."

Chapter 16

The next day the taxi driver transporting Simon and me up the hill to the former gynecological hospital spoke enough English to provide a minor sightseeing monologue, pointing out the railway tracks where Jews were assembled to board the cattle cars of deportation and the nearby former Jewish cemetery, which an open-air market had rendered undetectable as burial ground for Jews. Depositing us at the entrance to the distinctively designed, but also very neglected, hospital building, he wished me "good luck, madame."

The waiting area of Dr. Sofia Zubko's office was a compact square lined with two chairs on each wall. No tables, no shelves, no magazines, no pictures on the wall, no health posters. When escorted there by what sounded like the same gruff assistant I had spoken to on the phone, Simon and I were the sole occupants.

"I haven't been in a gynecologist's office since the Jolly Janet was pregnant," said Simon, invoking his sarcastic nickname for an insufferable ex-wife, the mother of his two grown children.

"Don't expect an outcome like that from this visit," I said.

"Do you want me to go in with you?"

"I don't know. If I were really here for a medical reason at this age, it would probably be a concerning one, like bleeding or some other symptom of cancer. Hot flashes don't qualify as anything a foreign visitor would bother with on a trip. I only said that on the phone, because it was the first thing that popped into my head. Then there's my daughter with problems . . ."

"I wondered about that. Why did you say that?"

"Maybe to indicate a problem a younger woman would have. I don't know. I was flustered, and these female gatekeepers have such off-putting phone manners."

"Madame Kovner, or should I say Mrs. Kovner? I am Dr. Zubko. Please come in. You, too, sir, if you would both prefer."

She offered her hand for a hearty shake before waving me into the corridor beyond the door. Simon followed us into her office, where a desk faced two visitor chairs placed about a foot in front of a curtained off space that I assumed was the examining area. The token personal touches were three Cyrillic diplomas on the wall and on the desktop a framed photograph of the doctor and a man, presumably her husband, standing behind a seated younger woman holding a little girl who looked about five.

The doctor's blonde hair tinged with strands of silver aptly matched the description we heard from Halina in the gallery; it was bobbed and framed her round face neatly but without much concern for style. She wore her white lab coat unbuttoned over a purple turtleneck sweater and black skirt that did not successfully conceal an abundant bosom and midriff roll. Matronly was the first word that came to mind. Grandmotherly. Our mutual grandmother, in fact. The doctor's resemblance to Bubbe took my breath away like the unexpected sting of the pretty red stuff—horseradish—I had too generously spooned onto my first helping of gefilte fish in this city nearly sixty years before.

If she noticed my reaction, which I did not think I disguised so well, she did not say. Ignoring Simon as well, she got down to business immediately.

"Now," she said, "you told my assistant you wanted a consultation both about hot flashes and about your daughter? I assume she's not the one having hot flashes. And why isn't it your daughter who has come to see me? You don't live here. I can't imagine hot flashes would bring you in during your travels, unless they just started. How old are you?"

This immediate and forthright attention to the business at

hand was exactly what I should have expected from a physician in a place and society in which the term "bedside manner" was likely an oxymoron. Yet, her barrage of questions conflicted with the disorientation I felt as I considered that, in this banal setting and situation, I had found a woman who might be my cousin. It took me a moment to pull myself together before answering. Simon held and squeezed my hand, a discreet sign of support.

"I'm sixty-five. And, no, hot flashes are not a problem for me."

"Then something else that you just didn't want to discuss on the phone? This business about your daughter?"

"Doctor, I see you are an open and blunt person. This is a quality I value, so I'm going to not waste your time. I will tell you why I'm here. I came because I believe we might be relatives. Might you have been a Jewish girl with the last name of Weinberg?"

It might have been my imagination or simply wishful thinking when I thought I detected a momentary startle and hesitation as she stared at me and then averted her eyes away before standing up and rebuking me in a voice dripping with scorn but tempered in volume in order to keep the words from carrying beyond the room.

"No, madame, I am not a Jew. I have nothing against Jews, mind you, but I'm not the person you're looking for. I'm sorry to disappoint you, if you're on what they call a Jewish roots trip. You should both get out of here right now."

We got up to leave. Simon had his hand on the doorknob when Dr. Zubko stopped us.

"Wait. Please tell me what in the world could have given you the idea I'm your long-lost cousin or any other relative. Who told you I could be that person? Who told you I could be a Jew?"

As I turned back to answer, I saw she was gripping the desk as if to ensure it would hold her upright. She looked chastened, even frightened. Again maybe my imagination.

"Apparently, you and I both had grandparents who had a painting by an artist named Anton Kozakiewicz. We visited a gallery with one in the window, not the same one as my grandparents, and the woman in the gallery told us you had said the same thing."

She relaxed a bit and said, "Kozakiewicz was a well known artist. Many people had his paintings. That was not such a great clue. Enjoy the rest of your trip, Mrs. Kovner, and . . ."

She turned to Simon and softened her face into a half-smile.

"Simon Rieger," he said as he laid a business card onto her desk.

"Mr. Rieger, forgive my rudeness when you came in. Yes, nice to meet you, too. Both of you. Enjoy your visit. Goodbye."

"We're staying at the George Hotel, by the way," he said.

"Charming," we heard before the door closed.

Back outside we walked down the slope to the main drag to find a taxi. A trolley car approached, but we had no clue where it was headed or how much to pay. A woman buttoning her coat over a nurse's uniform waited at the trolley stop and heard our confused wonderings about whether or not to get aboard.

"If you want to go to the center of Lviv—Rynok Square area—this is a good train to take. It is only a few *hryvnia*. I will tell you when to get off."

She paid our fare. When we thanked her profusely and Simon offered her a few dollars, she demurred.

"No need," she said. "We are happy to see foreigners here. I hope you were not at the hospital because you are ill."

"No," said Simon, "just doing an errand for an old friend."

"That was a clever line," I said when we got off and waved goodbye to our latest transport Good Samaritan who, unlike the loquacious Leonid of the previous day, performed her helpful deed without benefit of compensation.

"First thing that came to mind."

"I'm glad one of us had presence of mind. I'm numb. That was my cousin. She looks just like my grandmother. Bubbe was such a warm and kind woman who loved me from the first minute she saw me. That was not my normal everyday childhood experience in Vienna.

Today I realized the memory of it must have been stored somewhere. Seeing the doctor—her face, her shape. She looks exactly like Bubbe . . ."

"Yeah," he said, "but the warm and loving part you've talked about is missing."

"She knew," I said. "I know she knew. She wanted to say something. Maybe she's scared. Maybe her position would be jeopardized. Her life here. That photograph on her desk must be her family. Husband, daughter, granddaughter. I'm telling you Dr. Zubko is my cousin, but she can't, or won't, admit it to me or to herself."

I started to cry. Tears that would soon freeze if we did not get inside the hotel soon.

"Well, if she doesn't want to acknowledge that, or can't, there isn't much more you can do. I wish there were."

When we entered the hotel, the concierge flagged us down in the lobby and handed me a thin nondescript white letter envelope.

"I'll open it upstairs," I said.

We got up to the room and took off our coats. I settled myself on the bed before ripping open the envelope. In it were two color Polaroid photographs: one showed the Kozakiewicz painting—my grandparents' painting last seen in Rome, not the pale specimen in the Lviv gallery—and The TaZ codex was on the other. Each was defaced with a thick black X crafted in Magic Marker. There was also a small piece of white scratch paper with a note that read, "It Could Happen to You and Your Cousin The Doctor."

Simon looked at the photos and said, "Oh, shit. The threats are intensifying. Probably The Duck. But how does the doctor fit into it?"

"And how does he know she's my cousin? He's either playing with me by taking advantage of my belief—my hope—that she's my cousin or inadvertently confirming it. And, if that's the case, how does he know? After today's visit we just can't barge back in and ask her if she knows The Duck. But I sure wish I could figure out how they're connected."

PART IV

Lviv, Poland, and USSR
1943-1948

Chapter 17

Magdalena, formerly Chanah, soon realized that the catechism and cross Auntie gave her were for show only. Although she bragged incessantly about her son in the seminary, Jadwiga never went to church. In fact, other than work at the hospital, she went practically nowhere and no one came to visit. This was a life style that probably made her the ideal caretaker for a Jewish girl who, despite her looks that could "pass" and her new name, really could not engage in such normal activity as going to school. Occasionally, she would go with Auntie to scrounge for whatever food, increasingly limited in variety and quality, was still accessible to the local citizens; rarely did Magdalena go anywhere alone for more than a few minutes.

After quickly absorbing all the books her real aunt, Freya, had sent with her, Magdalena found herself poring over Auntie's medical books. Chanah had loved science and math in school, and Shlomo had teased her about these not being girls' subjects. School and her brother were part of the past she had to push out of her mind in order to survive as Magdalena. Despite her restricted and mostly homebound existence, she was constantly on guard.

Two months after she moved in, the sainted Pawel came home for a visit that Auntie anticipated with great excitement. Magdalena was mildly curious to meet this young man, whom she thought looked serious but not unattractive in the head shot in his black seminarian garb. She was surprised to see that his physique was short and stumpy. More shocking, though, was his appearance in a very different black outfit: the uniform of the German-controlled Ukrainian Auxiliary Police, the *Ukrainische Hilfspolizei*.

Auntie was shocked that her son had apparently abandoned his religious studies. In turn Pawel was astounded by the presence of this young woman stranger now living with his mother and occupying his bedroom. He glared at Magdalena throughout the welcome dinner that Auntie tried to make festive by serving the two prized commodities he brought, a fresh goose and a bottle of authentic German Riesling. Such bounty apparently came with the privilege of Pawel's new position.

The running water she used to clean the dishes did not drown out the argument between mother and son that ensued right after Magdalena left the table. Pawel minced no words in the interrogation.

"Who is this stupid girl? What is she doing here? Where am I supposed to sleep? You're hiding a Jew, aren't you, Matka? I know you. Heart of gold and all that crap. The caring nurse."

"Pawel, no, absolutely not. Calm down. Magdalena is the daughter of my cousin from Krakow. Poor Agnieszka died when the child was a baby. I told you this. Now the father is dead, too, in the war."

"I thought you told me the baby died, too."

"Oh, no, I don't know how you got that idea. This is Magdalena, the sweet baby almost all grown up. But an orphan. My flesh and blood. Agnieszka and I were so close. Don't worry about your room. She can sleep on the sofa while you are here, if you want. She's a good girl, she won't mind. Don't be upset with me, Pawel. These are not normal times. And what about you?"

"What about me?"

"You didn't tell me you joined the police. How could you just leave the seminary? You would have been ordained in another year."

"I wanted to be patriotic, help out our brave Ukrainians. The seminary is a bore. It's never been the life I really wanted. I just went into it to please you. Now even you don't go to church."

"The war is too exhausting. And work. It is better to stay home these days. After the war I will go to church, and maybe you will go back to seminary."

"Don't count on it."

"Where do you live?"

"I live in a barracks a few kilometers from here. Beyond the camp Janowska. That is where I my job is."

"What do you do in this job?"

"I help the people concentrate on their work. I keep them safe that way. It's God's work in another method of doing it."

"I don't exactly understand," said his mother, "but it sounds important."

"Did you get anything for taking this girl in? Any money? Where did that ugly picture come from?"

"Magdalena brought it. It's not ugly; I like it. A famous Polish artist painted it. I admired it when I used to visit Agnieszka's house in Krakow. The girl remembered that and brought it when she came."

"Well, the gold frame must be worth something, at least."

Magdalena understood only too clearly that Pawel must be a guard or enforcer of some type. Hardly the religious scholar and future pastor of his mother's grandiose boasts. The former Chanah had permitted herself some sense of comfort and security since she had moved in with Auntie. But the conversation she heard brought back a disturbingly familiar anxiety related to her true identity. She hoped Pawel would not stay long, even though he magnanimously told his mother the girl could stay in his room and he would sleep on the sofa.

In the middle of the night she did not hear the bedroom door open. But the touch of a cold hand on her breast underneath her nightgown startled Magdalena into opening her eyes to find Pawel kneeling alongside the bed. Terrified, she pushed his hand away, pulled the blanket up to her neck and tried to cry out but was stifled by his hand now cupped over her mouth.

"Shut up, you Jew girl," he said. "If you know what's good for you,

you will let me do whatever I want with you. Or I can take you to the camp right now. Or even shoot you."

"I'm your cousin, Magdalena," she said. "Your mother won't like this."

"My mother is a fool to think I believe her that you're a cousin. And you are a fool to think she did this for nothing. How much did you pay her to take you in?"

He yanked the blanket away and roughly squeezed a breast with one hand and pinched an upper thigh with the other before standing up and stalking out.

"I'll be back for more," he said.

Although nothing like this had ever happened to Chanah, she was not completely naïve. Her reading of love stories and the menacing scenes she had witnessed on the streets informed her in two very different ways that this was neither desirable nor romantic treatment from a man. Pawel was in a position to violate not only her body but also her safety. If she told Auntie, would the mother even believe her? Pawel was still her son, despite her apparent dismay at his career change. If Magdalena somehow managed to resist him, perhaps by physically striking or even biting him, he would surely denounce her to the Nazis. He had the power to treat her however he chose. His visit was supposed to last only a few days. They promised to be tortuous.

The next day Pawel rose and left the house early. When he returned he brought a beef roast, a big cake, and another bottle of wine, as well as a silver cup that looked to the former Chanah like a Kiddush cup made by an artisan whose wares her parents sold in their shop. It was engraved in a grapevine pattern and dotted with pearls. He presented it to his mother as a gift.

"Where did you get it? It's beautiful."

"From someone I know at the camp who is going away and isn't going to need it anymore."

"Going where?"

"To a better place."

His mother asked no more questions, and Magdalena certainly didn't either. Then he extracted from his suitcase a dark red leather-covered book that was closed with a silver clasp; it looked like an oversized diary. His mother asked him what it was.

"Oh, it's a book with some Jew writing on the pages. I got it just for you, sweet little cousin. You can read it, can't you?"

He pushed the book toward her on the table and said, "Read it."

Magdalena pushed it back.

"I can't read that. Why would I know how to read those letters?"

Auntie, very distressed, told her son to stop acting so terribly.

"This is my cousin. I've told you that. She is my responsibility, and I won't have you making accusations that are ridiculous. Just because you've become a Nazi doesn't mean this is a Nazi house. Where did you get that, anyway? From another friend?"

"The big synagogue on Staroyevryeiska Street. The Germans finished it off today, and I found this book just lying on a pile. It might be worth something—the fancy leather cover and this silver clip. Nicer than an average book. Maybe I can even sell it. But the cup I want you to have, Matka."

Magdalena recognized the location of the demolition as the Golden Rose Synagogue. Though heartsick at the thought of the magnificent temple in ruins, she had to act like it did not matter.

"Maybe we can go there this week, Auntie, to see if there's anything else of value we can find at that place," she said.

"It's been picked pretty clean," said Pawel. "Don't bother."

When Auntie excused herself early because she had an early hospital shift the next morning, Magdalena hoped she could stave off the son by immersing herself in sewing the hem of a dress she was lengthening. Pawel announced he was going out to meet his pals drinking. Magdalena took his departure as her cue to try to figure out how to erect a barricade against the bedroom door. She did not change into a nightgown and tried to stay awake in an effort to fend off whatever might happen later. She finally dozed off after midnight.

Pawel, even weakened by drink, proved strong enough to invade her homemade fortress. The difficulty he had in opening the door followed by his anger at discovering her fully dressed only served to exacerbate the level of violence he used to attack Magdalena. This time it was rape that left her ripped and bleeding and with bruises strategically delivered onto areas of her body that would be concealed by clothes.

By the time Magdalena struggled out of bed the next morning, Auntie was long gone to work, and Pawel was gone, too. He returned sporadically every few weeks during that late summer and autumn of 1943, dropping in without advance notice for a night or two of terror in the bedroom, threatening every time to turn her in as a Jew. One night he forced her to lie on the leather book from the synagogue. That was only a minor perversion in his twisted repertoire. The sole saving grace of Pawel's behavior was that he no longer voiced to his mother his objections to Magdalena's presence or his belief that she was Jewish. Auntie was relieved her son had accepted her guest and blithely assumed they had achieved a relatively normal family life, despite the tension and privations of the war. She still nagged him about returning to the priesthood but gladly accepted the tangible perquisites of his new career serving the Nazis. From Magdalena's perspective the single shred of value Pawel and his line of work brought to the household was information about what was happening to the Jews of Lwów.

Shortly before Christmas Magdalena heard Auntie's end of a telephone conversation that ended with an especially enthusiastic and loving sign-off with her son.

"Pawel's camp has been closed," she said, "so he left his barracks two weeks ago and returned to the seminary outside town. Now the priests there have given him some special assignments that will require him to travel—even to Rome. But he doesn't have to leave until January. Isn't that great? He will be coming home for Christmas and the New Year and a real stay. Not just a short one- or two-night visit."

The news of the camp's closure, along with Pawel's previous report about the liquidation of the ghetto, meant the city was nearly drained of Jews. Magdalena, inured to exile from her family and community, could no longer register any mental surprise or tangible anguish. Conversely, but not without a minor tinge of guilt, she considered this devestating reality an opportunity to escape the relentless sexual attacks. If most Jews were either dead already or deported to their likely deaths elsewhere, perhaps there was less activity focused on apprehending them. This proposition, shameful as it might be, emboldened her; anticipating weeks of nightly torture broke through her malaise.

The next day, when Auntie was at work, Magdalena left the house carrying just a grocery basket on her arm and a small rucksack on her back. She figured the central business district of the city was safer than any of the residential neighborhoods. Auntie had always insisted she carry a small amount of money for emergencies that might arise on her infrequent outings. It would not last long but got her on the trolley.

Arriving downtown, she noticed the city streets were more deserted than the last time she was out, and there were fewer German soldiers in evidence. Those who remained seemed tired and enervated; their uniforms were less crisp and forbidding; most loitered about smoking while leaning against buildings or aimlessly kicking the ground. The occasional citizen rushing by, bundled in a soiled and threadbare coat, paid no attention to them. Shops were either closed or lacking in anything to display, despite the approach of Christmas.

This bleak picture panicked Magdalena about what to do next. Then, edging along Rynok Square, she spotted a sign in the window of the Black Eagle Pharmacy. It read, "Assistant Wanted, Lodging Included." A job? A room? Could she, only fifteen years old—sixteen on her identity papers—qualify for this?

She entered the old, legendary business and waited until the middle-aged gentleman behind the counter finished waiting on a woman carrying a bawling and coughing baby. She approached and asked politely about the job and lodging.

"Young lady," he said, "how old are you? Do your parents know you're looking for a job?"

Magdalena surprised herself with the fabrication she came up.

"Yes," she said. "I need to work. My father came home from the East with a serious injury. He cannot walk or talk. My mother is a nurse but cannot work all the time, she must take care of him. They took in a lodger to help with expenses, so there is not enough room for me. I must strike out on my own."

"If your mother is a nurse, perhaps you have some familiarity with medical terms and drugs?"

"I have read a lot of medical books, and science classes were my favorite."

"So, you're not still in school?"

She did not know how to answer because, as a Jew, of course not. But were Christians still going to school? She had to venture a guess.

"Our school was shelled and not repaired."

"Yes, things like that have happened," he said. "This war has changed everything. Our business. Our staff has either moved to the East when the Nazis came, or have been moved by the Nazis, if you understand what I'm saying. Our supplies of medication and chemicals are very limited, but we have to do all we can to help our customers. If your papers are good, you can have the job. You seem like a smart girl, but I don't want any trouble."

She withdrew Magdalena's papers from the grocery basket. He looked at them and looked at her and handed them back.

"I will show you the room, Magdalena. My name is Leonid. I have worked here for many years. Welcome to the Black Eagle."

The room was a tiny, windowless garret where Magdalena had to crouch down just to get into the single bed. The only other piece of furniture was a small bureau, and a single bulb provided poor light. One sink and toilet on the way upstairs from the pharmacy served employees and customers, and that is where she had to manage her ablutions. Even at Auntie's the accommodations were nicer.

Yet, at that moment—and for days, weeks, and months that passed quickly afterward—she felt relief for escaping Pawel, as well as hope that the diminishing Nazi presence on the streets and Leonid's surreptitious reports on war news meant it would end soon. Uncle Nathan and Aunt Freya would come back to collect her or send her a ticket to meet them in Palestine. She could be Chanah again. Until then, she had work where she was stimulated and appreciated, even praised. Leonid, her boss entrusted with the run of the place by the absentee owner, treated her well and with increasing respect as she quickly soaked up on-the-job knowledge and skills related to drugs and their uses.

Her major fear was that Auntie or, worse, Pawel himself would show up and drag her back, and in general she never left the pharmacy without anxiety that her real identity would catch up with her. Only once, strolling back to the pharmacy from buying some bread and cheese, was she temporarily caught off-guard when she happened upon a posse of German and Ukrainian police noisily extracting, one by one, a trio of what they called human "garbage" from the sewer at the end of the street. One sodden and filthy girl, trying to yank herself out of the grip of a manhandling, uniformed thug, yelled out.

"Aren't you Chanah? Chanah Weinberg?"

She knew it was Sorel Stolnick, a long-forgotten friend from school.

"Sorry," she murmured, "my name is Magdalena."

She walked away as quickly as possible, fearing that either running or Sorel's persistence, or both, would inspire the captors to pursue her. Turning the next corner, back in front of the pharmacy, she heard three shots. But no one followed her. Silently, she blessed Sorel's memory.

In the summer of 1944 a Ukrainian nationalist uprising against the Nazis foreshadowed the arrival of the Russians. Leonid closed up the pharmacy early on the day of a particularly violent melee in the streets and rushed Magdalena out of there to stay with his sister, who lived

167

in a fortress of a building a few blocks on the other side of the Latin Cathedral. As she and her boss zigzagged around the square to avoid getting caught up in the rioting crowd, she felt a fleeting instant of dread when she spotted Pawel dressed as a priest and cheering in front of the cathedral. When the Russians liberated the city soon after, she no longer thought about him or Auntie. Other than work, she focused on reuniting with her family.

Chapter 18

The week after V-E Day, in May 1945, a Russian officer came into the pharmacy and introduced himself as the new chief professor of surgery at the Lviv National Medical University. Magdalena immediately recognized him as Colonel Zagoravich, who had helped her parents sell off their Judaica inventory and, more significantly, had taken her father and brother with him into his departing convoy ahead of the Nazi invasion. Although she yearned to find Chaim and Shlomo and hoped the colonel could help her, she caught herself as she opened her mouth to tell him who she was. Her current status still depended on her identity as Magdalena. The Nazis were gone, but no Jews had returned, a fact that told her being openly Jewish was still unwise. Anyway, four years older, now an adult, she thought it unlikely he would remember her at all.

After a short talk about new treatments for infection, he asked Leonid to introduce him to the staff, which had grown to five after the war. When it was Magdalena's turn, Zagoravich fixated on her with what she perceived to be a look of recognition.

"Charmed," he said. "Young lady, are you planning to remain here at the pharmacy? I doubt you were able to finish your schooling during the war, but perhaps you would like to pursue more studies. Even in medicine."

"Perhaps," she said.

"If you would like my help in securing a place at the medical university, please contact me. I do not have a new calling card yet. If someone has something I can write on, I will give you my number."

Leonid, gratified that the colonel also saw potential in his young protégée, quickly handed over a small piece of paper and a pencil. Zagoravich passed the note to Magdalena on his way out. She tried to look casual when she opened and read what the colonel had written in addition to a phone number.

"George Hotel at six tonight. Call if not possible."

At promptly six she walked into the hotel. The colonel beckoned her to the chair next to his in the lobby and spoke almost in a whisper.

"Chanah Weinberg, I bring you news of your father and brother. Unfortunately, it is not good news."

The pleasant sensation of being addressed by her real name again passed quickly when she heard all the news he was able to report.

His convoy had taken Chaim and Shlomo to Odessa, where they lodged first with his relative, then with a Jewish lawyer of impeccable Communist credentials. The trip was physically punishing for Chaim, who suffered a heart attack the day after they arrived and mercifully died before the infamous Odessa Massacre the Nazis perpetrated a few months later to retaliate for Soviet bombings that killed Germans and their Rumanian partners in their murderous sweep through the area. Shlomo had delusions of joining resistance fighters but he had to keep running to stay alive. Chanah's brother trekked northward to Minsk, where there were underground activists known to be welcoming, or at least accepting, of Jews. Ultimately, the colonel learned, Shlomo and his mates were captured and strung up in a forest.

She nodded throughout the saga but did not cry.

"I want you to come and stay with my wife and me," the colonel said. "You can matriculate at the faculty of medicine. You have talent. You should resume your education as soon as possible."

"Only until my aunt and uncle come back for me," she said. "Then I will go to Palestine and study there."

"Of course."

"Do you have any way to get information about them?"

"Perhaps."

"Would you please go to Anton Nowakowski, Uncle Nathan's business partner? Maybe he has information."

A week later later the colonel came to the pharmacy and asked Leonid if he could take Magdalena out for coffee. Her boss already knew his young protégée would soon matriculate at the university under Zagoravich's tutelage, and had given his blessing.

They sat down at the nearest café. The colonel told her that things were not good for the Nowakowskis. Anton had briefly been accused of collaborating with the Nazis for the factory's manufacture of German uniforms but had been acquitted by the testimony of one surviving Jewish laborer. Like other ethnic Poles in Lviv, he and Stefania were moving to Poland.

"And about my aunt and uncle? Have they heard anything?"

The colonel reached across the table and took her arm, a sign, she figured, he was bracing her for bad news. All Anton knew, he said, was Nathan and Freya remained unaccounted for among the inmates of Bergen Belsen. Sadly, he said, some Jews still resided there, and in other concentration camps, but not as Nazi prisoners, just as displaced persons. Stateless.

"But Aunt Freya and Uncle Nathan wouldn't be stateless," she said. "They have Palestine passports. They should have gotten to Palestine even during the war."

What Zagoravich did not have the heart to tell her was he had learned from Anton that the Weinbergs had not, in fact, been among the few hundred Jews ultimately exchanged for German Templars. Instead he promised to keep checking through his own official channels and to stay in contact with the Nowakowskis.

Within a few weeks Magdalena was ensconced in her own room and en suite bathroom in the sumptuous quarters of the colonel and his wife, Tatiana. Magdalena had never encountered anyone quite like this wisp of a woman who chain-smoked, ate little, and consumed, without obvious adverse effect, an incongruous amount of vodka for a woman of her size. Her streetwise practicality and caustic sense of humor sometimes belied the empathy she had for her guest. But Magdalena liked her from the start and also suspected they shared the secret of a Jewish background. This was never confirmed.

Magdalena was too ashamed and shy to discuss her experience living at Auntie's with the colonel. After a few weeks in the Zagoravich household, she did confide in a horrified Tatiana, who told her husband that night the Magdalena identity had to go.

"First," said the forthright Russian woman, "because she got that name in a terrible place. Second, it's Polish. She needs to be Ukrainian or even Russian to get ahead here now."

By the time Magdalena Wolski, née Chanah Weinberg, attended her first class at the medical university, she was registered as Sofia Zubko. She inherited the birth certificate of a country girl who was shot straight into a ditch in the forest outside Rohatyn, seventy-five kilometers from Lviv, as retaliation for partaking in an ambush of a convoy of German soldiers under the command of one Rudolf Bucholz. Hundreds of innocent Rohatyn Jews were condemned to death for the same act.

PART V

Lviv, Ukraine
1995

Chapter 19

Shortly after Simon and I buried the subject of the disfigured photographs, there was a knock on the door. When he opened it, Sofia Zubko, in a stylish grey tweed wool coat, stepped in tentatively, projecting herself more like a sheepish adolescent than the direct and commanding figure who had washed her hands of us only a few hours earlier. I got up and welcomed her, literally, with outstretched open arms but waited for her to speak.

"You're Lily Weinberg, my cousin from Vienna, aren't you? I am . . . I was Chanah."

"I know."

We embraced and cried.

"Sit down, doctor," Simon said. "Can I order up something to drink or eat? Or would you like to go downstairs to the bar or dining room?"

"No, no, not at all. I can't stay long. I have to get home. My husband will wonder where I am. Besides, truthfully, and I'm ashamed to say this, we can't be seen together in public."

"After what you told us this afternoon in your office," I said, "I'm delighted but confused. I knew it was you but I didn't think you wanted any part of me or of the past. Why did you come? What made you change your mind?"

She reached into her purse and pulled out photos of the codex and painting cut and marked exactly like the set I had received. The message on hers read, "It Could Happen to You and Your Jewish Cousin from America."

"Do you know who sent this? Who The Duck is?"

"The Duck? What are you talking about? I know who sent this, but who or what is The Duck?"

"Kaczka. The Duck in Polish. That's the name of the so-called priest who has the codex and the painting."

"Kaczka. Very funny. Yes, I get it. The Duck in Polish. But that's not the name I know him by, which is Pavel Zelenko. Ukrainian. His mother did always call him Pawel, the Polish way. She was Polish from Krakow. Maybe Kaczka was her name before she was married. Yes, it's certainly the same person, and now he's a priest again."

"Forgive me, but now I'm confused," said Simon. "What are you talking about?"

"Zelenko. Kaczka. One and the same man, one name Ukrainian, the other Polish. A chameleon. Or schizophrenic. Like Lviv itself: its name has changed with our shifting borders and invaders. Whichever side is up, you adapt to it at any given time. With the Nazis and the Communists it was better to be Ukrainian. With the Roman Catholics back, Polish is at least as good, like before the war, when this really was Poland. Even I have had three names. As for calling him The Duck, I know him, and, believe me, I cannot find any humor in the joke or anything else about him."

"How do you know this man?"

"I have known him for more than fifty years. And he has tormented me the entire time."

I had not yet absorbed the shock that Sofia had reversed course, sought us out, and confessed to be Chanah. Now her unfurling story might turn out to hold the key as to why Simon and I had even come to Lviv.

"Tormented you? What could you possibly mean by that?"

"First by sexually assaulting me as a girl when I lived with his mother. Later by blackmailing me. That continues to his day."

Her statement jolted us. Sickened, I got up and hugged Sofia again. So many Holocaust stories were grisly and difficult to tell and hear, but I could never be immune to the revulsion of yet another one. Eager, and afraid at the same time, to hear more, I addressed the most benign part of what she said.

"You lived with his mother? How? Why? Where were your parents?"

As soon as the words slipped out of my mouth, I knew what a stupid question that was. I had seen the Yad Vashem report. Chaim and Esther were listed as victims of the Holocaust.

"My parents left me early. And my brother. Do you remember I had a big brother, Shlomo? My father had a friend, a Russian medical officer, who offered to take us, our whole family, to escape safely with him to the Soviet Union before the Germans came. My mother wouldn't go. She couldn't decide what to pack, she just couldn't get up and leave in a matter of hours. My father begged her. It might not have saved us, but at least we would have been together. In the end he and Shlomo went. I would have gone, too, but I was too young to make the decision for myself. No one asked me. The decision was made for me to stay with her."

"And then you and she . . ."

"Within a few months after the Nazis came, they began to build the ghetto. They came to our house one day when she was home alone—I was at Aunt Freya's house. Freya and Uncle Nathan. Do you remember them?"

I nodded.

"My mother had hired a moving cart to take our belongings to the ghetto. Can you imagine such idiocy? As if we were moving to a nice new house. The cart followed the truck they loaded her on. We were told that when she got to the ghetto, she argued with an officer about the small space she was allotted. So he shot her. I stayed with Freya and Nathan. He still worked with his original business partner in the clothing factory, which the Nazis commandeered to make soldiers' uniforms. After a while Uncle Nathan heard there was a plan to trade Jews with Palestine passports for Germans living in Palestine—the Templars—and he and Freya had traveled to Palestine years before and had obtained those passports. They knew his partner Anton couldn't shield him indefinitely from being deported, so that special deal sounded like the best way to leave. I didn't have a Palestine passport, so they couldn't take me. They tried to keep all these details from me at the time, but I knew and understood more than they thought."

"As I did." I said, "when my mother was trying to get me on the kindertransport and she thought it was a big surprise when she told me the day before that I was going to visit my aunt and uncle in London."

My cousin shot me a look that could charitably be called exasperated.

"At least she didn't leave without you," Sofia said bitterly. "At first I heard them saying, in their bedroom at night, they would never leave me. Then they talked to me about how, with the special treatment and passage to Palestine, they would come back for me soon and we would all be eating oranges off the trees in the Holy Land. But their first stop was going to be Bergen Belsen concentration camp, which didn't sound like such a special deal to me. Anyway, with my blonde hair I never looked typically Jewish; even before the Nazis it was a joke in the family—a joke I didn't like—that I looked like a little *shikseh.* You see?"

We could only nod. There was nothing to say.

"So I could pass. I could be left. Everybody left me. No one came back for me. And still I pass."

She pulled out a tissue from the purse on her lap and dabbed her eyes gently. Her face softened up again as she almost smiled when I reached for her hand. I dared to ask another question.

"Who was The Duck's mother, and how did it happen that you went to live with her?"

Sofia said, "Jadwiga. She was someone Anton and his wife knew. A nurse in a hospital. It wasn't her fault. She didn't know what Pawel was doing to me when he came home to visit. First, when I moved in, he was away studying to be a priest. Then he was in the Ukrainian

Auxiliary Police, local Nazi scum. Just before the war ended, he was supposedly going back to being a priest and told his mother he was going to travel on important assignments for the Vatican. That's when I left. He was coming home for two weeks' holiday before going to Rome; I couldn't abide two straight weeks every night. Next time I saw him, after the Communists took over, he wore the uniform of the Ukrainian security force. Now he says he's a priest again. But my latest payments I sent through the post. That's real blackmail. Talk about a bad joke."

Simon had said nothing while listening to her astounding story but now took an audible deep breath.

"Blackmail all these years," he said, "after what he did to you? He's still extorting from you?"

"The whole time—first the abuse of my body, then money."

"Why? What does he hold over you now?"

"That I'm Jewish."

"Still, today," I said, "with the Nazis gone and the Communists gone, that would be a problem for you?"

"Even my husband and daughter don't know I was—I am—Jewish. I never took another religion. Just two new names and identities."

"Why two?"

"Like The Duck I played the game or the game was played for me. Under the Nazis I had the very Polish Catholic name of Magdalena Wolska. The Red Cross people laughed when I went there after the war and asked if any deported Jews who survived were looking for me. 'With that name and your blonde hair, you're not Jewish,' they said. And, of course, I no longer had my Chanah Weinberg papers. Later the Russian doctor who had taken my father and Shlomo came back and helped me get into medical school. A good Ukrainian name would be useful, he said, and that's when I became Sofia Zubko. I also thought a new name would help me escape Pawel. But he came to work in the security detail at the university, saw me, and immediately figured out my new identity."

The Jewish thing nagged at me.

"Really? Coming forth as Jewish is still a problem?"

"When you're Jewish, and when you're me, you keep your head down, do your work, go home to your family. It would rock the boat. My position at the hospital, the leeway I get for the work I do with abused women. That all comes from my reputation as a physician. And also from respect for my husband's position . . ."

"What does he do?"

"He is a judge. I met him when we were both students. He is held in high esteem for the reforms he is bringing to the judicial system in the new Ukraine. Even now an openly Jewish wife would not be an asset. You would call it politically incorrect."

"His name is Zubko, too?"

"No. Andryi Pachko. He is a good man. We have one daughter. In my heart she is named after my mother. Not Esther, of course. Nothing so Jewish. So she is Elizabeta. She is a history professor. She is divorced, but she has a daughter, Yulia, who is eight, and the apple of my eye."

"My daughter is also named Elizabeth," I said. "After my mother. She has a little girl named Charlotte. My son, named Jacob after my father, has boy and girl twins, Gabriella and Joshua."

Sofia turned toward Simon and said, "You're not the husband of Lily?"

"My husband died almost seven years ago," I said. "Simon and I have been together for about five."

"But, really, what are you doing here in Lviv? How do you know about the scoundrel you call The Duck? Pawel, Pavel?"

Simon said, "I was asked to look at the codex—that is the book with the red cover in the photos. It is supposed to be a previously unknown work of a famous rabbi here, The TaZ. It was brought to Rome by The Duck, which is the nickname used by the priest who showed us the codex. On the day we were supposed to meet The Duck, the other priest turned up dead, and the codex was gone."

"Pawel brought that book to his mother's house. He said he got it from the rubble of the Golden Rose Synagogue after the Germans destroyed it. That fancy red leather cover and the silver clasp—that's what appealed to him. I'm sure he never opened it up, except when he taunted me with it and dared me to read the Hebrew. It was all such a pity. The Golden Rose Synagogue was especially beautiful, the showplace of the Jews here for hundreds of years."

"I vaguely remember you wanted to take me to see it when I was here with my parents and you told me the story of the girl, the Golden Rose," I said.

"Yes, stupid child that I was," she said, "I believed that legend of the heroine who saved the temple. Our own hometown Queen Esther. When I first went to Auntie's house . . ."

"Auntie? You mean Aunt Freya?"

"No, Jadwiga, Pawel's mother. That's what she wanted me to call her. I was Magdalena then, with the papers of some dead little cousin of hers in Krakow. Pawel was suspicious from the beginning when she told him because he thought she had told him the baby had died. From the first day he came home and saw me there, he accused her of harboring a Jew. But, about the Golden Rose—for a while I fancied myself like her, a heroine sacrificing myself for the survival of the Jews. Imagining how she felt when she went to the Jesuits to plead the synagogue's case. Brave, entrusted with an important responsibility, suffering for it. The only thing I accomplished was saving myself."

"But you were brave. To be left in a strange home with the Nazis all around you. To take a stand against the abuse Pawel inflicted. To get up and leave. To be a doctor offering care and shelter to other victims of abuse. That takes courage anywhere, but in a political and social environment like this? Your life has counted for so much."

She shook her head in response.

"Your opinion of me—my nobility—is touching but not accurate. I live a lie. I've not only allowed myself to stay hidden. I've lied and scrimped to do that, paying off a criminal simply because I'm afraid revealing my true heritage might compromise my nice way of life. You know how I find the money to send to Pawel? My husband has always known my salary; when he started to question why I was sometimes short on household money, I told him I'm giving it to the poor women I take care of. What kind of woman lies about doing good just to protect her own name?"

"You're too hard on yourself," I said.

She put up her hands in protest, and her expression indicated she would never be convinced. Enough.

"But you two still haven't told me why you even thought to look for me here," Sofia said.

"In the place where the priest in Rome had stored the codex I saw the painting your parents gave our grandparents for their fiftieth anniversary."

For the first time Sofia laughed.

"You mean the one that started the big fight between the brothers? The one your father called 'bourgeois?' Aha! Now I understand why you asked me about that Polish painter when you came to the hospital. Pawel's mother loved that painting. It came with me when I moved in with her. My parents took it after Bubbe died. It was left in our apartment when the Germans took my mother, so Freya and Nathan brought it to their place. Freya joked that maybe your father was right; even the Nazis didn't like it enough to steal."

"My father shouldn't have spoiled that party, though," I said. "He was such a snob. About you all, about being Jewish. He was so arrogant and often very cruel to my mother, though not to me. Ironically, he was the first casualty of the Nazis in the whole family."

"Served him right," Sofia said. "No, I'm sorry. I take that back. No one deserved that. None of them, not our family or the rest of the six million Jews or all the others killed in that war."

"Did you ever find out what happened to Nathan and Freya? Why they didn't come back for you?"

"No. I figured they were both killed. Do you know anything?"

I went over to my closed suitcase where I had stashed the report from Yad Vashem. I sat down again next to Sofia and pointed to the relevant spot on the list. She read it and looked at me.

"Nathan died at Bergen Belsen. But Freya lived to record all this information. She apparently remarried. Yet she never came for me? I don't believe it. She loved me like her own. I suppose she has died by now, too."

"Yes," I said. "We confirmed that through the Israelis. Maybe because of Soviet rule it was impossible to track you down? Your name changes? I'm sure she tried."

"I will always wonder."

We all sat silently for a few moments. Then, looking exhausted, she pushed herself up from her chair and put on her coat.

"Now I must go home. I am glad I came, but it has been long enough."

"Will we see you again?"

"Perhaps. You're still looking for The Duck and the codex. That's why you came. I cannot help you or get involved. I never see him. I send the money to a postal box. I don't like the situation but I like not seeing him."

"But he threatened you today, just like he threatened me."

"I'm used to his threats. All he wants now is money. He's a fraud and an all-around evil bastard but not a murderer."

"Lily suspects he poisoned the priest in Rome," said Simon.

"Like me with the Golden Rose," she said to me, "you have a graphic imagination. I'm glad we have met again after so many years, but please don't try to contact me."

She shook my hand and put her other arm around me in a half-hearted hug. It seemed untoward to respond more ardently.

She walked out and closed the door behind her.

As usual Simon offered the best suggestion as to what we should do next.

"Let's go downstairs and eat," Simon said. "It's too late and too cold to go searching around for a restaurant other than the hotel."

"First," I said, "the bar."

Chapter 20

The next morning we slept late until the phone woke us up at ten o'clock. Simon answered.

"What? Sofia? Yes, of course. Give me your address."

He hung up.

"She wants us to come over to her house right now."

"What? She acted like she might never care about seeing us again."

"I know. This sounds urgent. She spoke very quickly. She almost hissed."

"Maybe she's found out The Duck is not so harmless?"

We were in a taxi fifteen minutes later. We knocked at the door of the apartment in a stark and boxy Soviet-era building decorated with Cyrillic graffiti on the outside walls. From the austerity of the building and of the apartment we soon entered we concluded Sofia and her husband had not corruptly profited from their highly placed government jobs.

Sofia opened the door and practically pulled us into the large living room where a little girl was seated with her mouth gagged and her arms tied to the back of a chair. Behind her, one hairy hand gripped a shoulder, and the other had a gun pointed at her beautiful blonde head. The hands belonged to a squat, bald man whose wire-rimmed glasses and black papal skullcap accessorized a long black vestment over which hung a thick chain and massive silver cross.

The Duck.

Here was a character we had almost mythologized in the past week.

The scene was totally menacing. But I was riveted by that child's face: it was the Chanah I had met nearly sixty years old.

"Yulia?"

Sofia nodded and indicated we should squeeze together on the sofa next to her. She tilted her head to the left of where The Duck held Yulia. On a scratched low table, next to an ashtray overloaded with butts, was the codex. Leaning on the wall behind it, the famously "bourgeois" Kozakiewicz painting I had last seen on the wall of the trattoria in Rome.

The Duck was in charge. The phone rang, and Sofia got up to answer.

"Sit down," he said. "Ignore it. Now, Mr. Rieger and Mrs. Kovner, one million dollars, and you get the codex, the painting, and the little girl," he said.

"You're crazy," said Simon. "First of all, the codex, if it's not forged, is looted from the Nazi era, which alone makes it sketchy. Secondly, even if it's not forged, that amount of money is ridiculous—it's simply much more than it's worth. The TaZ was not exactly Moses, or even a Talmudic scholar as renown as Rashi or Maimonides."

Simon's rational, businesslike approach to the demand may have been appropriate, but at the moment it seemed incongruously sane. While I wanted to laugh out loud at the vintage Simon line about The TaZ and Moses, it did not amuse The Duck.

"You think you can bluff your way out of this, Mr. Rieger," said the ersatz holy man. "Keep going, and young miss Yulia will never laugh again. Now, I know there are many rich Jews who would love to buy this for the Israel Museum, no matter how important it is, just to put their names on the label. The museum can front the money and get paid for it afterward. The sooner the better."

"It doesn't work that way," I said. "The codex has to be authenticated and its ownership verified before even the richest of benefactors or museums would buy it. There may be a family from the Golden Rose Synagogue or even the heirs of The TaZ himself entitled to own this."

"No one gets it for free," said the Duck. "But the longer you stall, the shorter the time is for this lovely young thing."

The phone rang again and again The Duck motioned to Sofia to stay seated.

He tightened his grip on Yulia's neck. She winced, kicked her legs, and wriggled her tightly bound arms but uttered no sound, saving her breath under the tape over her mouth. This was a tough little girl worthy of her grandmother.

"Please, Pawel," said Sofia, "let her go. Tie me up. Take me away with you. I'm begging you. Haven't I paid you enough over the years? You're a priest. How much money do you need? What for?"

"Shut up, you dried up old Jewess. Who even wants you now? This one, who looks like you when you were a young maiden. She's another story. If I were even ten years younger . . ."

"Let her go now," said Simon getting up from the sofa.

The priest aimed, and a shot rang out. Simon grabbed his lower leg from which blood flowed. Sofia grabbed a green knit afghan next to her and gave it to me to bind it on him as a tourniquet.

"You see," The Duck said, "I mean business. Next time I will aim a little higher or just down here."

He pointed the gun toward Yulia's heart.

"Okay, now we understand what the deal is. A million dollars. That will top off the pittances you have given me all these years, Magdalena or Sofia, or Chanah, your real Jew name. Then I can leave this frozen hellhole once and for all. After what I did for those Nazis—getting them out of Europe—what was in it for me? They treated me like a delivery boy. Those big shots I took to Rome. Got them new identities, papers, passage. They made fortunes in South America to go with what they stole during the war. I helped them open Swiss bank accounts. Even Father Stash. He sent me on all those thankless journeys, and I asked him for one little thing after all these years: get the Jews to pay me now. They should be grateful I got those Nazis out of Europe. And he tells me no, it's not the right thing. We're men of faith. In his old age all of a sudden he really finds something in religion called morality or a conscience? Well, he paid for that. Strongest vodka ever."

Again the phone rang and again The Duck told Sofia to ignore it.

Yulia looked perplexed when The Duck called her grandma a Jewess. If the child got the drift of the sexual overtones, she did not let on, and I fervently hoped she was oblivious to it. As for the rest of the raving, it was such an amazing confession that I could not even sort out what entity or country would begin to have jurisdiction. Whether or not any would bother to prosecute was another issue.

A new voice said from the doorway behind us, "The Jews should be grateful for the Vatican ratline? Now there's a truly novel theory."

We turned around and beheld Jacobo Basevi, our friend from Rome, enswathed in an elegant black coat with beaver collar. In one leather-gloved hand, he, too, brandished a gun. In the other he waved a thin piece of paper that appeared to be check.

"Here is your million dollars," he said. "You will get it as soon as you untie that little girl and let her out of the chair. Then you will give me the codex and disappear, Father Kaczka or Zelenko or Duck, whoever you are. Nazi, Communist, thief, murderer. You will have money for your personal ratline to join your clients in South America or wherever.

Simon, wincing and pulling tightly on the now blood-soaked afghan, turned to Jacobo, who had moved next to our sofa, and said, "What are you doing here? And why would you pay this crook?"

"The codex is for my Zosia. Now do it: untie her."

"I will take your money or any Jew's," said The Duck as he pocketed his gun and began to untie Yulia.

"Sir, you can keep your money," said yet another new voice behind us.

"Andryi," said Sofia to the speaker, a dark-haired man with a thin nose and pointed chin, wearing round tortoise-shell glasses and a black padded coat and walking into the center of the room. "Why did you come? How did you know what was going on here?"

"Mama," said a pretty thirty-something woman, yet another blonde but this one with her father's features more prominent than Sofia's. "I called and called. You didn't answer. You told me you and Yulia were spending your day off together staying home to bake. When you didn't answer, I was so worried I called Tato."

"And I have brought my friend the Colonel General," said Sofia's husband the judge, bringing into the room the highest ranking officer of the Lviv Patrol Police who, in turn, directed his sergeant to collar the still ranting priest.

"Once a Jew, always a Jew," The Duck said to Sofia, as he was led away. "Why don't you tell them all about yourself, Chanah Weinberg?"

Sofia shrank into the sofa. She covered her eyes to avoid the gaze of her husband and daughter. Andryi sat down next to her and opened his arms. As she melted against him, he spoke to her.

"I knew, Sofia. I have known for a long time. About who you were— who you are—and I always suspected someone had abused you before we met. The blackmail and the money I only figured out recently. My darling, I can't believe you felt the need to conceal it all from me. I have always hated seeing you so obviously burdened and I hate myself for not doing enough to relieve you of your internal torture, for not even letting you know it was all okay, that you could trust me."

"I'm so sorry," she said. "I felt I could never take the risk of confiding in you, that our life together would fall away because of me. I was so ashamed of it all. Letting it happen—what he did to me—and then being such a coward about saying anything. I tell my patients it's not their fault but I didn't take my own advice. I didn't want to accept victimhood. Or abandonment. When no one came back for me, I just thought the safest thing was to forget about being Jewish. My family had all forgotten about me. I needed to forget about them."

"You see, dear," he said, "they didn't all forget about you. Here you have your cousin who has come all this way and you've found each other. The irony is that something wonderful—this reunion—came about because of The Duck and all the pain. It's all over now; he will no longer be in any position to have a hold over you. You—we all—can move forward without fear."

Sofia looked over to the wall and seemed to perk up.

"Another thing that brought us together," she said, "is that ugly painting, thanks to the gossipy Halina at the art gallery. What do you really think of it, Lily? Personally, seeing it again at this age I agree with your father. *Oy*, my parents and Nathan and Freya would have my head if they heard that. Do you want it?"

I shook my head.

"Neither do I," she said. "What do you say we give it to Halina and let her try to sell it?"

"Great idea," I said. "And all the proceeds will go to your women's clinic and shelter."

Simon cleared his throat and pointed to his leg.

"First," he said, "Doctor Sofia, would you mind taking a look at this?"

She knelt in front of him, unwound the afghan, and pronounced the bleeding stopped.

"It's just a superficial grazing," she said. "Look, there's a bullet fragment stuck in the upholstery. I can just clean and bandage this. The sofa is another story."

"We can get a new one," said her husband.

"Yes, from my leftover salary that will no longer go to The Duck. I guess we deserve a treat."

"First," said Andryi, "you will formally introduce us to your cousin, and we will make plans to celebrate tonight."

Sofia put her arm around my waist.

"This is my cousin Lily Kovner, Lily Weinberg Kovner and her friend, Simon. They live in New York City and Israel. Lily's father and my father were brothers. Before this week we only met once before, when our grandparents celebrated their fiftieth wedding anniversary. We are the only members of that family who survived the Holocaust.

Elizabeta, you're a historian; you have researched that horrible period. I could tell you so much about what it was like to have lived it as a Jew, even a hidden one. More importantly, you need to learn about the wonderful people in your own family who would have been so happy to know you and Yulia. My parents, my brother, my aunt and uncle, the loving grandparents Lily and I had. I promise to make this up to you, so you know who I really was, who I am, and who you can proudly be."

We had almost forgotten about Jacobo, who stood on the other side of the room cradling the codex in his arms. I could tell he had unfinished business he needed to set straight. As we did with him. When Sofia started treating Simon's wound, the Italian came over to us.

"I am so sorry you got hurt," he said to Simon, "but I'm glad it's not serious. And I want to apologize if you think I took advantage of meeting you in Rome. Zosia and I sincerely enjoyed the time we spent with you. I need to explain that this codex has been such a searing pain to her all these years. Like me with the *Fosse* Ardeatine."

"I don't understand the connection," I said. "Why?"

"The real Golden Rose was her ancestor who married into the Nachmanowicz family. Her own family always contended that she was mercilessly sacrificed for the glory of keeping the synagogue her husband's people built."

"Jacobo," said Simon, "do you and Zosia even know what is in the codex? It's written by The TaZ, the rabbi at that time. How do you even know it has anything to do with the Golden Rose, the woman, when it was simply something found in the debris at the synagogue?"

"Simon, you know yourself. It's a palimpsest."

Sofia piped up while intently cutting a piece of gauze.

"What is this word, palimpsest? I have never heard it."

"It's a manuscript or page with writing over previous writing underneath that remains somewhat visible, despite attempts to erase it," Simon said.

191

Sofia put down the scissors and gauze and rocked back on her feet considering this.

"I understand. Like me," she said. "My life is a palimpsest. Now the truth underneath has been revealed, no matter how hard I tried to blot it out."

No one spoke while digesting that comment until Jacobo gently addressed her.

"Signora, you are as noble as the Golden Rose. My wife Zosia seeks the truth, what's underneath the words of the rabbi, The TaZ. In her family it was always spoken of as the key to what happened to Rosa. It's worth a million dollars to her and, therefore, to me. She lost so much. It's what I want to do for her."

"And," said Simon, "when I told you about my work with texts and going to Lviv, you decided I might lead you to the codex?"

"When I met you in the ghetto," Jacobo said, "I suspected why you were in Rome, even before our conversation the next day. And then I kept up with your journey here to Lviv. At least as far as the codex is concerned. Your family situation, Lily, I knew nothing about but I am so happy for you and your cousin."

"You mean," said Simon, "striking up a friendship with us in the café was no coincidence?"

"Did you ever think that your masters in Israel employ other part-time experts? The ratlines, Swiss bank accounts. We all have our specialties, Simon. In Rome it's no longer much of a secret who in the Vatican was involved. One of the last survivors was your Father Gajos, no saint, believe me . . ."

"Father Stash? I guess I'm not surprised," I said. "Simon, didn't even Father Kaz at the Latin Cathedral tell us there were rumors about Father Stash among the next generations of priests?"

"Yes."

"Many of the younger, more reform-minded priests are horrified by this history," said Jacobo, "and they have been some of my best sources. Unfortunately, the scoundrels in the Vatican have always been untouchable, and many have already died. Father Stash was killed by The Duck, whose double or triple lives outside the Vatican gave him no such immunity. On behalf of the Mossad I've been looking for him for years. He was a seemingly penny-ante guy who participated in some major international criminal activity during and after the war using his shifting identities and loyalties as cover to get away with them: a priest in the Catholic church, a member of the Ukrainian auxiliary police Nazis, a Soviet security official . . ."

"And a sexual predator and blackmailer," said Sofia.

"Yes, signora, that, too. I am sorry you have suffered such treachery at his hands. But with all this, the fact that he had the codex that my wife has wanted so badly—well, that was a bonus that just came along after all these years on his trail."

"Why did you introduce yourself to Lily and me in Rome? Did our mutual Israeli friends tip you off about me—that I was there to see the codex?"

Jacobo smiled and made a hand gesture one might stereotype as signature Jewish or Italian—or both—then reached into his pocket and produced his mobile phone.

"Think about it, Simon. Who else but one of us runs around the world with one of these? Mossad special. Now, go on and get bandaged up and enjoy your celebration with Lily and her family. I have a plane to catch with this codex in my brief case."

Epilogue

Israel

March 1996

On the invitation of Jacobo and Zosia, Simon and I were invited to join them and the small group of curators and museum officials that assembled in the Conservation Laboratories of the Israel Museum in Jerusalem.

Michael, the scholarly but affable head of Paper Conservation, had everyone sit down on stools around the table where the pages of the codex were laid out. He wore gloves and handled it gingerly.

To restore the six-page book to any kind of legibility, he said, required the intensive application of conservation procedures one would expect after its perilous journey from presumed three-hundred-year safekeeping in the Golden Rose Synagogue into the rubbish pile of the Nazis' desecration and fire to Jadwiga's home and wherever else The Duck lodged it, with a side trip to Rome and the back room of Franco's trattoria. He did not have to spell out for us, he said, the lack of proper care and conditions for preservation of any of these settings. There were some tears to the brittle pages reparable by parchment glue. The ink of the Hebrew on top was considerably smudged but not enough to completely obliterate the meaning and intent of The TaZ to whom it should be accurately attributed.

"The palimpsest," Zosia said. "Can you tell what's underneath?"

Indeed he could. The efforts to erase the writing underneath the one page where it was found were, fortunately, amateurish enough that modern techniques using ultra-violet light could reveal almost completely what was there. A team of linguists and historians from the Hebrew University had come in to translate and interpret that portion.

"It's a mix of Polish and Yiddish," he said, "so the letters are both from the Latin alphabet with elements on top and the Hebrew alphabet. The professors told me it might have been written in haste, but with eloquence and correctness. They found it absolutely astonishing that a young woman of that time would have been so literate."

"What does it say?" the museum director asked. "We want to announce the acquistion of this astounding piece and the wonderful gift of Mr. and Mrs. Basevi. The TaZ was a renown scholar, and this is one of the first notable recovered pieces from out of the former Soviet Union."

"Well," said Michael, "the disciples of The TaZ may not like it. He may have been a great scholar, but this does not reflect well on him. It will be controversial."

Aha! Finally, the perfect story for the free-lance assignment my editor friend Marty had given me five years before. Former Soviet Union Judaica, controversy.

But before I could find the time to sit down and write it, I had guests arriving. Sofia and her family stayed with me for five days in Jerusalem, and we spent another four at Simon's seaside villa. One day, with Yulia and "Uncle" Simon happily enjoying a schedule of pool, beach, and ice cream, I drove Sofia, Andryi, and Elizabeta north to a cemetery near the sea at Nahariya. The keeper accompanied us on our walk along aisles of dry grass barely passable between rows jammed with the coffin-size grave markings typical of Israel. Finally, he pointed to the one we were looking for. It was inscribed in Hebrew, Polish, and, unaccountably, English. We asked if he knew why.

"According to the instructions she left, which we have in our file, in case a relative who didn't read Hebrew ever visited. The lady wrote she had lost track of someone behind the Iron Curtain since the war."

Sofia wept and placed on the grave both a bouquet of flowers and a stone, the traditional Jewish symbol of remembrance. With her husband and daughter beside her she read aloud:

Freya Weinberg Zusman (born Rubin)
1899-1992
Daughter, Sister, Wife, Aunt

Appendix

The TaZ Codex

(Translated and interpreted from Polish, Yiddish, and Hebrew in retrieved but fragmentary sections, including (1) a letter to Rabbi Isaac Ha-Levi (approximate date 1608), a chief rabbi of Lemberg, revealed despite attempted erasure and (2) an address to the Lemberg community (approximate date 1653) by Rabbi David Ha-Levi, author of Turei Zahav, "Rows of Gold," for which he became known as The TaZ; he was the half-brother and a successor as chief rabbi of Rabbi Isaac).

Beloved and revered rabbi,

This letter bears the truth, and I pray for your merciful response.

My name is Rosa Bracha Nachmanowicz, born Levitzki. I am the widow of Zalman, son of Izak, the founder of the family synagogue. I was my husband's second wife whose five children resented me. They falsely said I gave him my maidenhood before our wedding and my golden hair meant my true father was a Christian. Zalman gave his children their mother's fine clothing, furniture, and jewelry. My own parents died leaving me without dowry but the duty to care for my two younger brothers. Zalman tried to shelter me from the abuse of his children. He built me a fine new house, gave me clothes and gems, more than I could ever dream of. He supported my brothers in yeshiva and welcomed them into our home for holidays. But after two years he took sick and died in a week.

My husband's oldest son sent me on an errand to the Jesuits, laden with a sack of gold coins from my accounts and my own jewelry, which he insisted I take. When I asked why, he told me the priests had issued a claim for ownership of the land under the synagogue. Money and gems would lead them to dismiss their petition. Why he did not go himself? This should be the obligation of a man. No, he said, your beauty and charm will add to the bounty in the sack. This was the first time he paid me a compliment.

I see now that was mockery. He tricked me into this mission. The bishop has confined me to a locked room opened a few times a day to permit me to empty my chamber pot into a trough in the gated yard. In those few minutes outside this cell, I receive a plate of vile food, mostly what Jews are forbidden to eat. The cook, a woman who does not speak or even smile to me, has dared to touch my hand gently to signal sympathy. Every night the door to my room is opened again. The bishop himself enters and forces me to his will in ways no decent man would inflict on a woman.

Last night the bishop told me the dispute has been settled, what I brought has more than satisfied the financial claim, and ownership of the land has been restored to the synagogue. But I must remain as the bishop's permanent hostage to seal the accord, a demand agreed to by the family. The bishop said my husband's family is circulating the story that I came here of my own free will to save the synagogue and that you, my beloved rabbi, are composing a Song of Deliverance that celebrates the return of the synagogue as a miracle of redemption akin to our people's return from slavery in Egypt and captivity in Babylon.

You celebrate. I am abandoned and sacrificed.

The ancients heaped jewels and coins and live animals onto altars of fire. We no longer practice this sort of sacrifice, but I feel like one of those animals or like Isaac being laid down by Abraham to die in the name of God. If I have saved the synagogue, a holy place, do I not merit salvation? In Proverbs we are told the Lord desires justice above sacrifice.

I will give this message to the cook to deliver to you. I beseech you to free me from this prison and the abhorrent treatment of my jailer. I ask no glory or gratitude for saving the synagogue. Only my own return to the community, where I would remain dedicated to righteousness. My hope for rescue rapidly fades. Soon despair will force me to end this torment. I walk already in the valley of the shadow of death. I do not fear it.

Rosa

My dear followers,

It is a rare occurrence when a young student has had the opportunity to learn at the feet of his brother throughout his life and it is rarer still to be chosen to step into the footsteps of that brother. I am humbled to assume the mantle of chief rabbi of this city of Lemberg. Sharing the name and the blood of your very esteemed Rabbi Isaac throughout my lifetime, it is an unbelievably sacred honor to now take the position that he performed so well. I pray that my service to you in this city and in this beautiful and hallowed synagogue will equal his, though I modestly declare this will be a high goal to accomplish.

I speak of this space, a gift to our community from the generous and honorable Nachmanowicz family. The patriarch built it originally to provide a private house of worship for his family, but the next generation shared its grandeur with all Lemberg Jews. When the Jesuits claimed a right to the land beneath this sacred place, and the king supported their petition, the family's crowning gesture of generosity and dedication to worship of God saved it for us all. Their precious Rosa, the daughter-in-law, took it upon herself to entreat the bishop to withdraw the Jesuits' claim. Believing that her fair looks and sincere heart would persuade him, she delivered there her own fortune and fine jewelry, despite the offer of the family to provide the financial settlement. That voluntary act of selflessness restored this sacred sanctuary of God's grace to us and to the Jews of Lemberg in perpetuity. Such a deed has been only equaled in our history when we were redeemed from exile in Egypt and Babylon and returned to the Promised Land. The Song of Deliverance, so magnificently created by my revered brother, Rabbi Isaac, gives praise for such miracles of survival.

What still confounds us is why this woman, this Rosa, felt it was her duty to choose to leave her people and remain with the bishop. Was there perhaps a trace of Christian blood that aligned her with the Jesuit spirit? Even as we question her motivation, we must never malign this departed sister, for the righteousness of her mission speaks for itself.

In my lifetime I have myself confronted the savagery of those who would prefer the end of all Jews. Violence and murder have forced me, along with my family, to flee Ostrog, where I had to abandon the yeshiva I established and the community I had long served as rabbi. I experienced the hatred and cruelty of the Cossacks who perpetrated these deeds on the Jews and I saw with my own eyes some of the atrocities in progress. Our history as Jews and our ongoing need to remain vigilant about those who would prefer to see us dead are reasons to constantly renew and continue our praise of Rosa. She took herself directly to an enemy of our people with the objective of saving this, our precious house of prayer, and our existence as Jews in Lemberg. Her mission and her memory are truly a blessing to us all.

We must never forget Rosa. She was our own Queen Esther, which is why we invoke my brother's Song of Deliverance on Purim. And I stand in awe of my brother, my teacher, who served as the leader during that most difficult time in the history of this place. My work has concentrated more on study and teaching. Leadership of a synagogue with such noble founders and a savior who inspires us is a task I undertake with open eyes and strength to confront the great challenge that lies ahead. I pray I am equal to it and that this place will remain a sacred home for all of us, not just during my personal tenure as chief rabbi, but for the many generations of Jews in Lemberg that will follow us.

I challenge, you, too, my fellow Jews of Lemberg, to join me in dedicating your lives and hearts and souls to prayer and good deeds. Together, as we always celebrate our good fortune to pray in this beautiful place, let us not forget the generous gift of Isak Nachmanowicz, whose blessed and righteous descendants sit with us every Shabbos joining us in mourning and praising their Golden Rosa.

Glossary of Foreign Words in
The Nice Little Blonde Girl

Bubbe:	Yiddish for grandmother
Di Goldene Royz:	Yiddish for the Golden Rose
Hryvnia:	Ukrainian currency
Kinder:	Yiddish for children
Kvell:	gush with pride
Lekach:	honey cake, tradition for Rosh Hashanah, the Jewish New Year
Mamzer:	Yiddish for bastard
Matka:	Polish for mother
Nu:	Yiddish question as in "what's new?"
Oy gevalt:	Yiddish expression of distress or surprise
Shaigetz	Yiddish for non-Jewish boy
Shikseh:	Yiddish for non-Jewish girl
Shul:	Yiddish for synagogue
Tata:	Yiddish for father
Tato:	Ukrainian for father
Zayde:	Yiddish for grandfather

Author's Note:
The Nice Little Blonde Girl
Was My Cousin

While *After the Auction* is based on stories of actual people and situations and *The Lost Torah of China* was inspired by my history and cultural interests, *The Nice Little Blonde Girl* mirrors a story in my own family.

They called her Haika, but her Hebrew name may have been Chanah, and she did become Sofia. She was born in Lwów, Poland, and her mother, who was my grandfather's first cousin, did indeed die at the hands of the Nazis when they opened the ghetto in their city. One story is she was pulled apart in front of her family, a scene I simply couldn't bring myself to write in the novel. Exactly when or how the father exited the picture I don't know. After their mother's death, Haika and her brother Shlomo were taken in by their aunt and uncle (their mother's brother David, fondly nicknamed "Dudu") who had a little girl of their own slightly younger than Haika. That little girl, now in her eighties, recalls being jealous of her mother fussing over the brushing and braiding of Haika's blonde hair and telling her how nice and well-behaved Haika was. Dudu worked in a business that afforded them protection for a while. There was also a single aunt, a sister of his and of Haika's mother.

The plan to exchange Jews for German Templars is not fiction. How or why my relatives thought they would qualify I do not know, except Dudu and his wife had traveled to Palestine in the 1930s to visit family members who had already made *aliyah* (settled in the "Promised Land"). They may have had authentic Palestine passports for themselves and their daughter. (Or not so authentic.) The single aunt and a man they knew posed as a married couple traveling with their "son" Shlomo. It was true that Haika was viewed as easiest to "pass" as a Christian, and she was left with a woman well compensated to take care of her. Haika was said to be "exploited" by the woman, and she left that house on her own while still a teen-ager. Maybe she was treated like a servant. Or was my fictitious sexual abuse not fiction?

Everyone else did go to Bergen-Belsen. They were not exchanged for Templars but survived and migrated to pre-state Israel in September 1945. After the war Dudu tried to locate Haika and reunite her with the family but was stymied by the difficulty of piercing the Iron Curtain. His brother, another uncle who had spent the war in labor camps in the Soviet Union, came through Lviv, found her, and wanted to take her with him. Reportedly, she would only go with Dudu, the one who had promised to retrieve her. He died in the 1960s, the promise not kept.

In the early 1990s, after the fall of the Soviet Union, Dudu's daughter went to Ukraine and renewed a relationship with her cousin, now Sofia, who was initially reluctant because she believed her late uncle and family had willfully abandoned her. Only upon hearing her cousin say "my father tried until his dying day to find you" did she soften. However, Sofia insisted on introducing her Israeli cousin to her family as "Cousin Alexandra from the States." Not until Sofia herself was terminally ill did she tell her children and grandchildren that she had, in fact, been a Jewish child and Cousin Alexandra from the States was really Cousin Sharona from Israel. Sharona was the child jealous of her mother's attention to the "nice little blonde girl" and the primary source of my knowledge about Haika.

I have met Haika's beautiful blonde granddaughters, her daughter's children: one lives in Israel with her Ukrainian husband and two small daughters; retrieving Haika's Polish-Jewish birth certificate enabled them to migrate there. The other, who lives in Lviv with her own young daughter, is a history professor. She questions some of Sharona's version and maintains the Soviets did not totally insulate Lviv from the outside world until a few years after the war ended. Therefore, it would not have been impossible for the family to find Haika. Her grandmother told her she had gone to the Red Cross asking if anyone was looking for her. Maybe the timing was off, as the family was displaced in Europe before reaching and getting settled in Palestine. Lack of documentation may have also interfered with Red Cross efforts.

Finally, there's a really wacky tale about the adult Shlomo who attended a professional conference in Moscow and set out by train to see his sister. He arrived in the company of two attractive Russian women and did manage to find Sofia. She freaked out at his foolishness: he could be cavorting with KGB spies who would reveal her Jewish identity to her government employers. Shlomo was forever banished from Sofia's life, though the Lviv granddaughter told me he told her mother that Sofia was Jewish even before Sharona appeared. When? Where? How?

In families no two stories are consistent. You can see why I fictionalized this one.

As for fiction vs. truth, there's the legend of the Golden Rose, the other blonde girl whose story is depicted in the palimpsest text. Long known as the heroine who saved the beautiful synagogue ultimately destroyed by the Nazis, the Golden Rose at least delivered the monetary bribe her family provided to the Jesuits. That is substantiated. Whether or not she sacrificed herself remains legend. There was indeed a Talmudic scholar, David Ha-Levi Segal, who became known as the TaZ and served as rabbi of the Golden Rose Synagogue. The palimpsest is, as far as I know, fictional, as is the character of Zosia as a descendant of the Golden Rose.

But no doubt the real family of the Golden Rose has at least a few versions of that story, too.

Acknowledgments

Obviously, cousins in Israel and Lviv have been the most helpful in providing the basis for this book, despite the inconsistencies in their versions. Sharona, Haika's contemporary, and Sofia's granddaughters Marta and Solomiya have all been equally forthcoming in sharing their memories. Marta in Lviv brought to our first and only meeting a treasure trove of photographs of her grandmother and other members of the family and insisted I keep them. I am very grateful.

The opportunity to take a private behind-the-scenes tour of the Israel Museum in Jerusalem in 2015 introduced me to the real Michael there: Michael Maggen, Head of Paper, Prints and Drawings Conservation. It was fascinating to visit his lab and hear about and see how he preserves and draws out the contents of written and pictorial treasures of various ages. I will never forget the story, both intriguing and heart-wrenching, of the restoration he was able to accomplish with the charred and fragmented remains of the diary of Israeli astronaut Ilan Ramon, who perished in the Columbia Space Shuttle. Subsequent correspondence and time spent with Michael taught me about palimpsests and how they are identified and "excavated." I am very grateful for this connection to a charming, patient, and gracious newer friend in Israel.

As I worked on this, the first book of the series mainly set in a place I had never traveled to before, I realized **location, location, location** is critical to my ability to visualize the plot. Fortunately, I was able to visit Lviv and environs, where my paternal grandfather came from, including the two nearby cities of Rohatyn and Ivano-

Frankivsk (formerly Stanislau, his birthplace in 1894). Our guide Alex Denisenko (aka, Alex Den) is a knowledgeable resource not just for getting around to the right places but also for the cultural and historical evolution in that area. Though not Jewish himself, Alex is a valued affiliate of Gesher Galicia, a non-profit organization carrying out Jewish genealogical and historical research on Galicia, formerly a province of Austria-Hungary and today divided between southeastern Poland and western Ukraine.

I was introduced to Gesher Galicia and to Alex by our mutual friend Marla Raucher Osborn, who leads Rohatyn Jewish Heritage (RJH). RJH develops and manages heritage preservation projects aimed at reconnecting the 400-year history of Rohatyn's now-lost Jewish community with the people and places of the modern Ukrainian city. I have spent time with Marla in three European cities she has inhabited as an expatriate—Paris, Warsaw, and Lviv. I so admire the dedication she and her husband Jay bring not only to recovering personal histories but also to restoring sacred spaces such as synagogues and cemeteries decimated by the Nazis. Their own tireless volunteer efforts and their ability to inspire others to join and support them are phenomenal. This work has been validated, and is now financially augmented, by the Fulbright fellowship recently awarded to Marla.

The process of writing this book lagged longer than I wanted initially due to indecision as to how to frame the story. Should I once again turn to my alter ego Lily and make this yet another "Jewish Miss Marple" quest? Or take this story out of the series as a one-off novel on its own? My trusted developmental editor Alan Rinzler helped me decide to run with Lily and worked through some of the process with me again. I appreciate and value his advice and friendship.

My family and friends continue to support my late-life fiction-writing career. Even so, between volunteer activities and a wonderful travel schedule, it's easy to find excuses to delay a book project. During the writing of *The Nice Little Blonde Girl*, there was a really great one: the birth of Mirah Elsy Ansfield, our first grandchild, in November

2017. Mirah already seems to be interested in books, and I hope she will someday appreciate the collected works written by her *Nainai*. Her parents Amy and Jonathan have been supportive and loving throughout the adventures of Lily, and the gift of Mirah blesses and enriches our family in new and wonderful ways.

Finally, my husband Eli, now also known as Mirah's *Yeye*, encourages me in all my pursuits, whether or not he thinks they are good for me. One thing he is always up for is travel: Go to Ukraine? Sure, why not?

I am very lucky.

Linda Frank
August 2019

Sources of Opening Quotations

Józef Wittlin, "My Lwów," translated from the original Polish by Antonia Lloyd-Jones, in Józef Wittlin and Phillippe Sands, *City of Lions*, London: Pushkin Press, 2016

The Book of Lamentations, in Rabbi Nosson Scherman, editor, *Tanach*, The Stone Edition; Brooklyn: Mesorah Publications, Ltd., 1996

About the Author

Linda Frank is a local and national volunteer advocate and leader retired from a business career. A lifelong passion for twentieth-century Jewish and world history motivated and inspired her first two novels, *After the Auction* and *The Lost Torah of Shanghai*. *The Nice Little Blonde Girl*, her third book, is based on a story from Frank's own family but unraveled through a fictionalized  plot because of inconsistent family reports about a deceased cousin. Journalist-protagonist Lily Kovner once again leads the action. As in Frank's previous novels, Lily takes the reader through another historical journey, this time in a place long embattled by changing rule and ethnic conflict.

In addition to her novels, Frank has written business, travel, and opinion articles for publications such as *The Asian Wall Street Journal, The Forward, Jewesses With Attitude* (a blog of the Jewish Women's Archive), and *Corporate Report Wisconsin*. She has also hosted her own cable television show that highlighted business topics, particularly as they related to women.